The British Invasion (the Bands) - The Best 60's Pop & Rock Music

An Uncompromising Deep Dive Into the History of Bands That Shaped Our Lives and Culture

P. J. Chambers

Dedication

"To the original 15th Avenue band members and sound guy. To Paul, Doug, Bart, Dan and Rob - the guys who jammed with me, gigged with me, cried with me and taught me how to stay in the groove and play the rock music I loved so much when we were just lads. Brenda the Fender is still alive and kicking! Bless you lads so very much."

(PJ Chambers, rhythm & lead guitar, keys and vocals - 15th Avenue band)

Contents

The 60's Were Groovy, Baby, Yeah!

The British Invasion certainly made a lot of noise in the record industry. –Jeff Barry (Songwriters' Hall of Fame—"Do Wah Diddy Diddy," "Da Doo Ron Ron," "Leader of the Pack")

The 1960s will forever go down in history as one of the most turbulent for many reasons. Everything was fast, and the music was groovy!

Part of not being square meant that you sported a Beatle haircut and indulged in the wacky sense of fashion while bookin' it in your bug, smoking weed en route to Woodstock.

This book looks at 10 British bands of the entire 60s widely agreed to be 'the best of the best'. Apologies up front to those who missed out. If you're looking for a sense of nostalgia when it comes to the music of the '60s that has shaped our lives and our culture, then this book is a must-read! You can expect to learn things such as:

- what happened in these ten bands' formative years
- how these bands changed the course of music history
- which artists were influenced by these music legends
- chatty facts and stats for the die-hard fans and newbies to the '60s music scene
- selected salacious details of their on-stage and off-stage antics

There's simply no denying that the '60s music genre, "the invasion" as they call it, belongs to the British. It was when the youth of America (and the world) succumbed to the sweet surrender of mop-topped musicians strumming rock and roll music on their guitars. But, it also speaks about the exotic and fresh vigor the songs brought, and with it, a pioneering new age in humanity and music as we know it.

While this book is everything it promises to be, what it's not is a tribute to just The Beatles (apologies up front). Of course, they gave the world Beatlemania, where millions of adoring girls abandoned themselves to complete hysteria, but many other notable bands have equally contributed (significantly at that) to the British Invasion. Some of the toughest, loudest, and rawest music the world has ever heard has come from the United Kingdom. Much to the dismay of some caring parents, we are all guilty of supporting these bands and their sometimes-delinquent tendencies. But it was a time when people were claiming freedoms, and the music was groovy, baby, yeah!

This book is about the "bands," while book two in the series is for solo artists. Also, importantly, this book covers what pop music-canon and opinion considers to be the 10 most influential British bands of all in the '60s, not just the wild, cultural phenomenon from 1964–67. Apologies again if your favorite British bands didn't make the top 10 of the '60s here, but check out the free

BONUS chapter to see if they made the top 20 (see the BONUS section at the end of the book). Hey! Send me feedback about where I missed it and what could/should be included in other books. I'd love to hear from you!

Even though this book is about the British bands that took over the pop-rock music scene in United States in the 1960s, some notable events and band stories will extend beyond into the '70s and after.

Specifically, we cover the band members of the '60s (with only some notables who joined these super bands in later decades and just cannot be omitted – you'll know who we mean when you read them.) The albums listed, and some of the hit singles, are (mostly) focused on '60s works; after all, that's why we're here! Where appropriate some later works are included demonstrating depth and influence of these simply awesome bands.

This book is a retrospective journey from a much-loved bygone era that is firmly cemented in the hearts and minds of many. It's a musical time machine that you'll enjoy, and it will take you back to a collection of memories that will bring a smile to your face and sometimes a tear to your cheek.

Are you ready to be transported back to the best of the best when it comes to '60s music? Then strap yourself in for a blast from the past like no other! This list of the top 10 bands and their stories will blow you away!

Chapter 1
#10 - The Animals

"To me, the Animals were a revelation. They were the first records with full-blown class consciousness that I'd ever heard." About the Animals' song 'We Gotta Get Out of This Place,' he was quoted as saying, "That's every song I've ever written...That's 'Born to Run,' 'Born in the U.S.A,' everything I've done for the past 40 years, including all the new ones. That struck me so deep. It was the first time I felt I heard something come across the radio that mirrored my home life, my childhood." –Bruce Springsteen ("The complete text of Bruce Springsteen's SXSW keynote address," 2012)

About:

The Animals were a music band that rose to prominence in the 1960s. They were known for their unique sound and eclectic influences, including blues, rhythm and blues, and rock and roll. The band members consisted of:

- lead singer Eric Burdon,
- keyboardist Alan Price,
- bassist Chas Chandler,
- guitarist Hilton Valentine,
- and drummer John Steel.

Despite, or because of, their success, the band was plagued by internal strife and disbanded (pardon that pun) in 1968. However, they reunited in the 1980s and continued to perform together until Burdon's retirement in 2013. Here is a look at the history of this iconic band.

Genre: Rhythm and blues, rock
Years Active in the 60s: 1962–1968

Discography:

Among their musical arsenal, they can count no less than 25 singles, 20 amazing studio albums, six compilation albums, and five fantastic EP releases. Some of them include the following:

Year	Album Name	Chart Position
1964	*The Animals* (Debut album)	UK #6 US #7
1965	*The Animals on Tour*	US #99
1965	*Animal Tracks*	UK #6 US #57
1966	*Animalization*	US #20
1966	*Animalisms*	UK #4 US #33
1966	*The Best of The Animals*	US #6
1966	*The Most/of The Animals* (1)	UK #4

The Band Members

Although there were various partial regroupings over the years, the original band members can be seen below:

Member	Position	Years Active	D.O.B	From
Eric Burdon	Vocals	1963–1968	May 11, 1941	Walker, Newcastle upon Tyne
Alan Price	Organ and keyboards	1963–1965	April 19, 1942	Fatfield, Washington (UK),
Bryan Chandler	Bass guitar	1963–1966	December 18, 1938	South Heaton, Newcastle upon Tyne,
Hilton Valentine	Guitar	1963–1966	May 21, 1943	North Shields
John Steel	Drums	1963–1966	February 4, 1941	Gateshead

Artistic Facts

- They started as a jazz group with Eric Burdon on trombone. It turns out Burdon was rubbish at playing the instrument so, they put him to better use as a vocalist and changed the genre to rock.
- Before settling on the name "The Animals," they were previously (but little known) as "The Pagans" and also "The Kansas City 5".
- After Chas Chandler left the band, he became a manager to Jimi Hendrix.
- The "New Animals" was joined by Andy Summers for a brief stint in 1968. Later, he would join "The Police".

- The Animals had many movie cameo appearances in the '60s. One such movie included *It's a Bikini World*. Later, after leaving the group, Price turned from musician to actor instead.
- Eric Burdon and John Steel met while attending the same school: Gateshead Grammar School.

Their Story

Over the years, many people have debated (and are still debating) whether the number one smash-hit single from The Animals, "The House of the Rising Sun," is the best folk song ever written. One thing is sure: When the originally dubbed band the Alan Price Rhythm and Blues Combo was joined by frontman Eric Burdon and rebirthed as The Animals, it catapulted them to stardom!

The Alan Price Rhythm and Blues Combo was formed in 1958 in Newcastle upon Tyne and produced many famous hits in the '60s era. They were well known among fans for their unique sound, which can only be described as the effective blend between American blues and British pop. In 1962, a massive change occurred in the band when Eric Burdon joined them, and the name change The Animals came about. It is thought that their new name was attributed to their acting like animals during performances. Still, Burdon denied this in a 2013 interview. OG (original group) member Steel stated in a 2021 interview that the name The Animals was bestowed upon them by one Graham Bond. Bond, in return, is credited as the founding father of the UK rhythm and blues boom.

It was none other than The Yardbirds' (see Chapter 5) manager, Giorgio Gomelsky, who convinced the band to relocate to London after reaching massive success in 1964 in their hometown with crammed back-to-back gigs. Luckily, this secured their spot in history as forming part of the British Invasion in the wake of Beatlemania (more on this later in the book).

In their '60s hey-days, the band was known for their wild onstage antics, especially from feisty Burdon, who boasted a powerful voice oozing with charisma both on and off stage. In addition, he has a very distinctive, deep crooner voice, which added to their charm. This magnificent band is one of the key players in the British Invasion of the United States.

June of 1964 saw them tour New York and even appear on the coveted *The Ed Sullivan Show*. They were escorted via a large motorcade with streams of adoring young gals shrieking from absolute joy at the mere sight of them. Sadly, as the tides of time ebb and flow, there were about as many changes to their lineup as certain people use toilet paper! Like any family dynamic, ructions started, and personal music preferences brought about many disagreements among the band members, so much so that Price decided to pursue a solo career in 1965 (with great success in the UK with a string of hit singles including "I put a spell on you", "Hi-Lili, Hi-Lo" and "The House That Jack Built"). Not only did he have a different vision for his life, but he also suffered from terrible aviophobia (fear of flying), so travel wasn't something he was open to. Mick Gallagher succeeded Price on keyboards, and Gallagher, in turn, was replaced by Dave Rowberry. Rowberry, in turn, was part of the band during the production of hit songs such as "We Gotta Get Out of This Place" and "It's My Life."

Before things ended in 1966, The Animals decided to part ways with their original songwriters, most of whom were recruited by Mickie Most under the Brill Building franchise. This was due to the band feeling that these songwriters doused the flame of their creative genius. They signed under the MGM Records label for the American and Cancuck regions and then with Decca Records for their record distribution in the rest of the world.

In 1966, Tom Wilson from MGM Records made and released an album with all the band's best hits and released it into the world. The album, *The Best of The Animals*, became their highest-grossing album in the United States. In February of the same year, fellow band muso Steel also left the band and was replaced by Barry Jenkins. Unfortunately, the biggest bummer came to pass in 1966 when the band members split up for good. The hit single "Don't Bring Me Down" was the last song released by The Animals. Apparently, due to all artists in that decade spending money like rain—and shockingly not earning that much money to start with—and due to theft from The Animals' then manager Michael Jeffrey, the band was disbanded for good. It is said that Jeffrey made the band work themselves to the bone and appropriated most of the funds for himself.

The year 1966 also saw Eric pursue a solo career, and he produced a solo album titled *Eric is Here*. One song on the record, "Help Me, Girl," became Burdon's UK #14 solo hit single, and this was subsequently his last released song with Decca Records.

However, Burdon was determined not to see his hard-earned success and howling voice go to waste. So instead, he assembled a band of fresh faces, and they called themselves Eric Burdon and The Animals. He moved his whole ensemble to California and even changed the genre to psychedelic hard rock instead of the smoky blues he was once synonymous with.

Eric Burdon and The Animals enjoyed 10 Top 20 hits on the UK Singles Chart and the US Billboard Hot 100 before the group was disbanded at the end of the decade. You can hear Burdon's distinctive voice on hit songs such as

- "The House of the Rising Sun" (1964)

- "Baby Let Me Take You Home" (1964)
- "I'm Crying" (1965)
- "Boom Boom" (1964)
- "Don't Let Me Be Misunderstood" (1965)
- "Bring It On Home To Me" (1964)
- "We Gotta Get Out of This Place" (1965)
- "It's My Life" (1965)
- "Don't Bring Me Down" (1966)
- "See See Rider" (1966)

Later, the OGs reunited for several quick comebacks, which included a benefit concert in Newcastle, their hometown, in 1968.

Our first top 10 countdown story has a fabulous ending that sees The Animals memorialized into the Rock and Roll Hall of Fame in 1994.

Legal Disputes

During the years, a fight broke out between OG drummer John Steel and Eric Burdon. In 2008, Steel was awarded the honors of owning the name "The Animals" in the United Kingdom because he filed a trademark registration. Burdon responded by rejecting the claim and said that he, himself, embodied any goodwill relating to the name. Eric's argument was rejected, as he had billed himself "Eric Burdon and The Animals" since 1967, thus separating said goodwill with his own name from the original band. However, Burdon did not give up easily, and on September 9, 2013, his appeal was heard (and granted), meaning he was now allowed to use the name "The Animals."

The Band Legacy

Even though The Animals were inducted into the Rock and Roll Hall of Fame, Burdon did not attend the event, and the band did not even perform. In a 2013 interview, Eric said that he could not attend due to work commitments in Germany at the time. He said that he was just told he was inducted into the prestigious honors, and that had been the end of the story. For a band with such a significant influence, it's pretty sad that he was told in passing and nothing more, don't you think?

Burdon and the original The Animals band later in 2003 released their rendition of "The House of the Rising Sun." The result? A coveted ranking (#123) on *Rolling Stone's* "500 Greatest Songs of All Time" list. Another song titled "We Gotta Get out of This Place" also managed to secure rank at #233 on the same list. Later, both of these songs formed part of the Rock and Roll Hall of Fame's "500 Songs That Shaped Rock and Roll" list, to be remembered in history for time immemorial.

Musical Influences

During a keynote address at the South by Southwest music festival on March 15, 2012, The Boss, a.k.a Bruce Springsteen, made a noteworthy speech about the degree of how The Animals influenced his music. He even credited The Animals as the inspiration behind his hit album *Darkness on the Edge of Town.*

The five-piece ensemble from The Animals also inspired Bob Dylan in 1965 to start working with musical groups and other artists who played electrical instruments in their songs. During Dylan's first album release in 1964, he added a version of the folk-blues song, originally by Eric Von Schmidt. The song "Baby Let Me Follow You Down" was renamed "Baby Let Me Take You Home" and boasted Burdon's distinctive rhythm-blues voice.

Later on, the keyboardist of the rock band Genesis (Tony

Banks) said that his idol, Alan Price, was the biggest musical influence in his life. He believes that Price was the first individual that made him think of using the organ in a rock repertoire.

Their Impact

The Animals were one of a few elite and leading UK-born and bred bands at the forefront of the British Invasion in the United States. American R&B as we know it today was heavily influenced by their songs. They had the uncanny ability to breathe new life into existing songs by injecting them with working-class toughness!

By the end of 1962, bands like The Animals flooded the American market with new-age British music sounds, which brought about a sense of musical openness. Their distinctive sounds and intricate musical ideas helped to internationalize the creation of rock and roll and opened the door for other artists and bands who followed suit. It can be said that due to musical influences from ensembles such as The Animals, late 1966 saw the end of pop music and the start of rock music as we know it.

Burdon himself has been credited for being the most considerable influence on the San Francisco psychedelic rock scene.

Top Quotes from The Animals

"Eventually, I would like to reach the stage where I don't have to write about love and kisses and all that stuff. I wish I could write about really ultimate things. That's where I think all of us want to go, really. All the groups seem to be heading towards a kind of pop music that deals with ultimate things." –Eric Burdon

"Well, it seems that one day Dylan was drivin' up to San Francisco from New Orleans or somewhere when our record [House of

the Rising Sun] *came over his radio. When it was announced, he said to Joan Baez -- who was with him at the time -- 'This'll be the first time I've heard this version,' although it was number one in the States. So he listened to it, stopped the car, ran round the car five times, banged his head on the bumper, and began leapin' about shouting, 'It's great! It's great!'"* —Eric Burdon, quoted by Clinton Heylin, *Bob Dylan: Behind the Shades: A Biography*

"I don't think Jimi (Hendrix) committed suicide in the conventional way. He just decided to exit when he wanted to." Eric Burdon ("The Animals - Famous Quotes and Quotations," n.d.)

Chapter 2
#9 - The Small Faces

A few years later, one of the LP's outstanding tracks, ... "You Need Loving," cropped up again to create rock history, albeit in a different format. "'Whole Lotta Love' by Led Zeppelin was nicked off that album," Marriott pointed out. "... We did a gig with The Yardbirds... and Jimmy Page asked me what that number was we did. "'You Need Loving,'" I said, 'it's a Muddy Waters thing'... After we broke up they took it and revamped it... until one day I thought, 'F***ing hell, that's us, that is. The bastards!'" –Paolo Hewitt (with a quote from Steve Marriott)

About:

If you're a fan of soulful British Invasion music, you need to know about The Small Faces. This band was made up of some of the most talented musicians in the industry, and their unique sound set them apart from the rest. Though they only had a short career, The Small Faces left a big mark on the music world.

Genre: Rock

Years Active in the 60s: 1965–1969

Discography:

Some of their top-sellers include 14 B-sides, a whopping 14 singles (all ranked), six studio albums, four compilation albums, and three live albums that still continue to thrill crowds world-wide. Some of them are the following:

Year	Album Name	Chart Position
1966	*Small Faces* (1)	UK #3
1967	*Small Faces* (2)	UK #12
1968	*There Are But Four Small Faces*	US #178
1968	*Ogdens' Nut Gone Flake*	UK #1 US #159
1967	*From the Beginning*	UK #17
1969	*In Memoriam*	-
1969	*The Autumn Stone*	-

The Band Members

Through the years they were active and thrilling the crowds, the band members consisted of the following:

Member	Position	Years Active	D.O.B	From
Steve Marriott	Guitar, vocals, keyboard, harmonica	1965–1969	January 30, 1947	Manor Park, London
Kenney Jones	Percussion, drums	1965–1969	September 16, 1948	London
Jimmy Winston	Keyboard, guitar, vocals	1965	April 20, 1945	Stratford, London
Ronnie Lane	Bass, rhythm guitar, vocals	1965–1969	April 1, 1946	Plaistow, London
Ian Mclagan	Bass, keyboards, rhythm guitar, vocals	1965–1969	May 12, 1945	Hounslow

Artistic Facts

- The origins of the band name is a two-parter. Firstly, it was due to all of the band members being shorter than 5-foot-6 (the "small" part). The "faces" portion of the name was inspired by a song done by The Who, titled "I'm the Face."
- Steve was a child actor turned musician. He portrayed the characters of both Artful Dodger and Oliver in an onstage production of *Oliver*.
- The Small Faces only had one #1 hit single on the charts in 1966, called "All or Nothing." They shared the position with "Yellow Submarine" from The Beatles.
- Did you know that after Ronnie Wood and Rod Stewart joined the band, the "small" was dropped in the band name? Since Wood and Stewart were taller, they decided, well... they weren't so "small" after all! They're not listed above, because a new band was officially formed! Tricky.

- After Lane was first diagnosed with multiple sclerosis, he briefly went into remission after his mercury-based tooth fillings were removed.
- Tragically for the world of music, Steve Marriott died in 1991 as a result of a fire in his home.

Their Story

This English rock band, founded in 1965, was one of the most influential and acclaimed modernist (mod) groups of the '60s era. They slowly evolved into one of the United Kingdom's best psychedelic rock bands during their successful stint.

Our story starts where Steve Marriott performed at a concert in 1964 and became acquainted with Ronnie Lane. However, it was only a year later, when their paths crossed again, that the two truly became friends. Marriott worked at J60, a music shop located in Manor Park, London. Lane was brought to J60 by his father, who bought him a bass guitar. Marriott and Lane struck up a conversation at the music shop, and soon after, Lane would visit Marriott after work to listen to records. Later, at this same music shop, the two friends met Jimmy Winston. The band picked up Kenney Jones while he played with Lane for a band called The Outcasts. After meeting Winston, rehearsals took place at The Ruskin Arms, owned by Ronnie's parents in Manor Park, London, and the band started performing regular gigs. This saw them get noticed, and soon they were playing at other pubs and semi-pro music events. They picked the name The Small Faces, and the rest is history.

The "face" portion of the group's name has a special meaning. Being a "face" meant something to them. It was a unique person with class and stature—someone who dressed sharp, possessed charm, and was a mentor to others (in addition to having the prettiest choice on their arm). It almost sounds like they were one of the very first versions of an Alpha male as we know it today.

The band enjoyed much success with their earlier R&B soul sounds, and this saw them perform covers such as:

- James Brown's "Jump Back" and "Please Please Please"
- Smokey Robinson's "You've Really Got a Hold on Me"
- Ben E. King's "Stand by Me"

Later, in the same year (1965), The Small Faces started performing two of their own original songs, penned by Marriott and Lane ("Come on Children" and "E Too D"). The latter provided Marriott with the perfect platform to show off his vocal prowess from his musical influences and mentors. His powerful voice made people sit up and notice, so much so that Elkie Brooks dropped the band's name in passing to a club owner called Maurice King. Needless to say, King really dug their music and immediately started sourcing gigs on their behalf.

Their first out-of-town trip took them to Sheffield at a working men's club. The primary audience at this club were rough and tumble local workers who worked hard and drank hard – and a sub-culture popularly called the Teds (Teddy Boys, or Teds for short). Teds were a sub-culture of youth devoted to the rock and roll music genre of the time, they also drank hard and could keep up with the local working lads. Unfortunately, the crowd did not take to the ensemble, and after only playing three songs, they were asked to leave. Down on luck, the band took their instruments, walked to the King Mojo Club, and asked to perform for free, which changed their music stars forever. The Mojo mods could not get enough of their unique sound, and the band was even supported by duo Sonny & Cher later that year.

The connection between The Small Faces and Sonny & Cher is particularly notable since the duo had just released two major songs, "Baby Don't Go" and "I Got You Babe," which shot them to stardom. So it was truly an honor to share the stage with the likes of them.

The band's first management contract was signed by Don Arden, which secured them a contract with Decca Records. Their first debut hit, titled "Whatcha Gonna Do About It," became a Top 20 UK Singles Chart hit. Unfortunately, their second single, "I've Got Mine," did not enjoy the same rave reviews as the first. The song was used in the 1965 Kenneth Cope film *Dateline Diamonds*, and despite Arden's gut feel, the single's official release had to be delayed. Even though the song received good reviews, it still failed miserably on the charts.

By this time (still in 1965), Winston decided he'd had enough and left the band. He enjoyed much success as an actor, solo artist, and even businessman. Much later, in 2000, in an interview, Kenney Jones said the reason that Winston was fired is that he believed himself to be better than Steve Marriott, which just wouldn't do. However, Winston had a different version of events, and in turn, he said he left because his brother and Arden were at loggerheads with one another. So, in true rocker style, we'll probably never know the real reason behind Winston's omission and replacement.

Enter Ian McLagan. Not only was he also short, but he had killer keyboard skills! His first official performance was on November 2, 1965. It seemed like when the band dropped Winston it also brought about the favor of Lady Luck smiling upon them. Their third single, "Sha-La-La-La-Lee," written by Mort Shuman, became a resounding success. This saw them embark on many successful tours of Europe and the United Kingdom and featured as regular guests on TV shows such as *Top of the Pops* and *Ready Steady Go!*

Later, their fifth single, "All or Nothing," hit the top of the UK Charts. According to Marriott's mum, he penned the song after breaking up with his then-fiancé, Susan Oliver. Subsequently, this song would prove their biggest blessing financially. But unfortunately, after the song's major success, it all fell flat pretty quickly. You see, the band was set to tour America with fellow bands such as The Mamas and the Papas, but Don Arden decided to pull the plug on the tour due to details of McLagan's drug conviction coming to light.

The saddest part of this story to date is that despite being 'outta sight' and enjoying much financial success in 1966, the band had very little money left over. Somewhere along the way Arden told the other boys' parents that the whole group was experimenting with drugs, and a major brawl ensued between all concerned parties. After the confrontation, The Small Faces decided to part ways with Arden and Decca Records.

During 1967 and 1968, the band enjoyed immense success by signing with a new label called Immediate, created by Andrew Loog Oldham (previous manager for The Rolling Stones). The Small Faces got to work and collaborated with their engineer Glyn Johns on their first single produced by Immediate. The single was titled "Here Come the Nice" and tells the tale of their journey with drug abuse. The most peculiar fact about the song is that it openly referred to a drug dealer dealing in the trade and did not suffer the effects of censorship. The second album, titled *Small Faces*, was not such a big seller compared to its predecessor. However, many other notable bands drew inspiration from the sounds produced on the record both in the United Kingdom and the United States.

Three weeks prior to the release of *Small Faces*, their ex-record label released an album titled *From the Beginning*. This was a beautiful marriage of both old and previously unreleased recordings from the Decca label. But their current management had dropped these tunes like a hot potato. The album brimmed with songs such as "My Way of Giving," "(Tell Me) Have You Ever Seen Me?", and their favorite on-stage song, "Baby Don't You Do It."

On August 11, 1967, the band released their next single titled "Itchycoo Park." This was the first of two singles to hit the charts in America, and it reached the #16 spot on the US charts in January of 1968. The single achieved a bigger status in the United Kingdom and made it all the way to #3. The Small Faces became the musical pioneers of the 'flanging' technique with "Itchycoo Park." This is a method whereby two master tapes are used simultaneously, but one tape is speed altered by gently touching the flange part of the tape reel. In turn, this produces a comb-filtering sound effect.

In December of 1967, the next Small Faces single was released, titled "Tin Soldier," and was penned by Marriott. Needless to say, it was fab. It enjoyed stints on the UK charts (#9) and the US Hot 100 chart at #73. The *Small Faces* album was later released in America but renamed to "There Are But Four Small Faces," omitting all the UK-produced record tracks.

In 1968, Immediate went against the band's better judgment and decided to release a song called "Lazy Sunday." The story behind Steve Marriott's inspiration is a pretty funny one! He wrote the song because he was in regular altercations with his neighbors—we mean, this guy's music is good, so neighbors, don't flip your wig! And it doesn't stop there. In the summer of 1968, another song was released titled "The Universal." This was recorded by Marriott's personal cassette recorder and even featured his pooches barking somewhere in the background. Unfortunately, the song failed to be a hit in the United States, and a disappointed Marriott decided to take a hiatus from his music writing endeavors.

Luckily, back home in the United Kingdom, things started looking up with the release of the band's record *Ogdens' Nut Gone Flake* in 1968. It not only featured songs with a strong psychedelic flavor, but the album cover was also unique back in the day—it boasted a round corner and was crafted to mirror an antique tobacco tin. It enjoyed six consecutive weeks at #1 on the UK Albums Chart but also failed in America.

The album contained a mixture of original songs on the A-side and fairytale-like songs on the B-side detailing the journey of "Happiness Stan". This character Stan went on many adventures in the two songs on the record in his pursuit of finding the other half of the moon, not visible from his standpoint. Music critics went ballistic, and the album sales were good. However, no good deed goes unpunished! *Ogdens'* was a masterpiece that was made in-studio, and for practical reasons, there was just no sure-fire way (at the time) where they could recreate this while on tour. Sadly, this saw the song only being done for one-night-only live on the BBC show *Colour Me Pop*.

In '69, all things came to pass, and Marriott made a dramatic exodus on stage (at a New Year's concert of all things) by yelling "I quit" and dropping the mic on his way out. Marriott's frustration was a culmination of the band's struggles to break out of the pop scene and produce unique pieces in the studio that couldn't be replicated on stage. It would seem that he was more discouraged at the failure of *Ogdens'* than what people realized at the time. Add to the fact that Marriott had already moved past The Small Faces and was looking forward to the formation of his new band, Humble Pie, in collaboration with Peter Frampton.

The world and the screaming girls felt the absence of The Small Faces after the band's breakup. Jones, Lane, and McLagan joined up with Kim Gardner, Rod Stewart, Art Wood, and Ronnie Wood to create Quiet Melon. They released four singles before Art and Kim parted ways with the band. This saw them rebrand the name to just "Faces."

Marriott and Frampton released their first single as the band Humble Pie. However, this wasn't enough despite reaching some success in both the United Kingdom and the United States, and subsequently, Humble Pie split in 1975. Not being one for giving up, Marriott went solo and released his first album in 1976.

The original Small Faces enjoyed a brief reunion stint in 1975. "Itchycoo Park" was turned into music videos and re-released, bringing the band back to chart status again. But as music trends and people change, Lane had parted ways with the band in 1973 following an argument. As it turns out, Lane had a closely guarded secret, unbeknownst to the other band members. The first symptoms of multiple sclerosis had started to manifest. The other band members thought that he was acting out in drunken disorientation, which was left at that.

The remaining three Small Faces stayed together and were eventually joined by Rick Wills in 1977, who replaced Lane. They recorded two more albums under the Atlantic Records label. During this time, the band was briefly joined by Jimmy McCullock as a guitarist who left the band Wings. Unfortunately, both of these albums were utter failures, and the band broke up for good in 1978.

Legal Disputes

In 2018, The Small Faces embarked on a mission to sue a West End musical that depicted the lives and times of the band members. Their reason was that the show was based on their lives and therefore claimed that they were owed at least £20,000 (US$26,216) as compensation.

It turns out that the band members were being paid royalties from the show before they launched legal action. However, the legal team for The Small Faces insisted they were to be paid more because of their reputations and images being used to tell the story. The show's producer, *EastEnders* actress Carol Harrison, didn't believe that the band was owed any more money.

Steve Marriott's estate manager, Chris France, said that the amount requested by the remaining Small Faces' band members was the least that Harrison could do after sponging off their name. A big legal battle ensued as Harrison's lawyers said they had sent a letter to the band's team saying that the band was already being paid royalties from the show and were owed nothing more than £300 ($401), if anything at all.

Musical Influences

Paul Weller (the '80s band The Style Council), Led Zeppelin, and Ocean Colour Scene have all cited The Small Faces as a major influence on their music.

The Band Legacy

In 2012, The Small Faces were inducted into the Rock & Roll Hall of Fame by Stevie van Zandt (once part of Bruce Springsteen's E Street Band) for their musical contribution during their stint.

There's no denying that any ardent '60s music aficionado will straight up tell you that these often underrated bands played a pivotal role in the history of the rock and roll genre. They were "small" in stature at first but could firmly stand their ground against more prominent bands (in height and record sales), such as The Beatles and The Who.

All their creative genius produced one-of-a-kind pieces such as *Ogdens'*, proving that the band was way ahead of their time, even though their tale is truly a tragic and often lonely one. They will go down in history as one of the most memorable bands of the flower power era but will probably never get the full recognition they so richly deserve.

Their Impact

The Small Faces was an English rock band from the mid-1960s. The group, who are considered one of the most influential mod bands, are best known for their hits "Itchycoo Park," "Lazy Sunday," and "Ogdens' Nut Gone Flake."

The Small Faces' music had a significant impact on society. Their songs captured the spirit of the mod movement, and their music was heavily influenced by R&B and soul music. This made their music unique and exciting, and it helped to popularize mod culture. The Small Faces also helped pioneer the use of psychedelic effects in rock music, and their album *Ogdens' Nut Gone Flake* is regarded as a classic of the genre.

The Small Faces' music was hugely popular during the 1960s and 1970s, and they are now considered to be one of the most essential mod bands of all time. Their influence can be heard in the music of many contemporary bands, and their songs continue to be popular with fans old and new. Thanks to their innovative sound and energetic live performances, The Small Faces have left a lasting impression on the world of rock music.

Top Quotes from The Small Faces

"I wore a kaftan for about two seconds. I regret it to this day." –Kenney Jones

"It was kinda half-baked. The concept should have run all the way through. I dunno what happened there." –Ian Mclagan regarding their 1968 concept album Ogdens' Nut Gone Flake ("Small Faces Fun Facts," n.d.)

"You don't just stop thinking about women because your wife dies. It's terrible, but you know. I just want the hugs, the kisses. A kiss!" –Ian Maclagan ("Ian McLagan Quotes," n.d.)

Chapter 3
#8 - The Moody Blues

Bands like The Move, Traffic, and The Moody Blues were proving that you didn't have to be from Liverpool to be successful –Ozzy Ozbourne (from Black Sabbath)

About:

The Moody Blues are known for their unique sound incorporating classical and psychedelic rock styles. They released several albums throughout the '60s and '70s before disbanding in 1978. However, they reunited in the late '80s and continue to tour today. Despite never achieving major commercial success during their original run, The Moody Blues have become one of the most influential progressive rock bands of all time. So put on your headphones and get ready for a trip down memory lane!

Genre: Rock

Years Active: 1964–2018

Discography:

Over the span of their enormous career, they released 27 compilation albums, 10 live albums, 16 studio albums, three video albums, and 36 singles. Their massive impact in the '60s came from these cracking albums:

Year	Album Name	Chart Position
1967	*Days of Future Passed*	UK #27 US #3
1968	*In Search of the Lost Chord*	UK #5 US #23
1969	*On the Threshold of a Dream*	UK #1 US #20
1969	*To Our Childrens' Childrens' Children*	UK #2 US #14

The Band Members

Member	Position	Years Active	D.O.B	From
Clint Warwick	Vocals, bass	1964–1966	June 25, 1944	Aston, Birmingham
Denny Laine	Vocals, guitar	1964–1966	October 29, 1944	Birmingham
Graeme Edge	Drums, percussion, vocals	1964–1966	March 30, 1941	Rochester
John Lodge	Vocals, bass, guitar	1966–1969	July 20, 1945	Erdington, Birmingham
Justin Hayward	Vocals, guitar	1966–1969	October 14, 1946	Swindon
Mike Pinder	Keyboards, vocals	1964–1969	December 27, 1941	Erdington, Birmingham
Ray Thomas	Flute, harmonica, percussion, vocals	1964–1969	December 29, 1941	Stourport-on-Severn
Rodney Clark	Bass, vocals	1966	November 23, 1942	Surlingham, Norfolk

Artistic Facts

- Thomas "poached" Hayward – he effectively diverted him from joining The Animals. Thomas somehow saw Hayward's response to an advert by Eric Burdon when The Animals were looking for new band members.
- The Moody Blues had their own record label, called Threshold. Threshold was a sister company of Decca Records in 1969. They signed on lesser-known bands and artists such as Nicky James, Providence, Trapeze, and Tymon. Sadly, Threshold made very little money for them.
- The band appeared in an episode of The Simpsons.

- Mike Pinder worked for a company that produced a device called the Mellotron. A Mellotron is a retro version of what we know to be a synthesizer. This piece of machinery is unique because it used tape loops to generate sound instead of electronic tone generators. This was an added bonus for The Moody Blues and produced their signature sounds.

Their Story

In 1964, The Moody Blues was founded in Erdington, Birmingham, United Kingdom. Ray Thomas, John Lodge, and Mike Pinder were all members of El Riot & the Rebels. The then-band was disbanded with one member going off to tech college, and Pinder deciding to join the army.

Pinder rejoined Thomas, and the band the Krew Kats was born. They toured Hamburg for a few months, and after the tour was deemed an utter failure, Denny Laine and Graeme Edge joined. Initially, Pinder and Thomas wanted John Lodge to join in the capacity of guitar player, but he was still at college, and this saw them recruit Clint Warwick instead.

Under the new band name, The Moody Blues, they performed in Birmingham in 1964 for the first time. It was initially speculated that the name came as a result of the five gents hoping for a sponsorship from the Mitchells & Butlers Brewery; needless to say, this never came to pass. The band also referred to themselves as "The M Bs" and "The M B Five" in a bid to draw the liquor giant's attention. In an interview much later, Pinder revealed that the actual reason behind the band's name was because he was tremendously taken with the fact that music changed people's mood and because the band started in the blues genre at first. During the same time, the band became regular performers at the Carlton Ballroom (later called Mothers).

The band's first UK-based management company was Ridgepride. This company was the brainchild of Alex Wharton, who worked for Decca Records at the time. The deal was signed, sealed, and delivered in 1964. The first single released was "Steal Your Heart Away," but like all things new, it didn't do too well. In the same year, they appeared on the TV show *Ready Steady Go!* debuting a song called "Lose Your Money (But Don't Lose Your Mind)." This song also failed to excite, but their second single, "Go Now," placed them on the map. This single (their only #1 single to date in the United Kingdom) was a hit and reached #10 in the United States. After the song's success, The Moody Blues decided to sign directly with Decca Records, following "management problems" at Ridgepride.

The band's debut album, titled *The Magnificent Moodies*, was released by Decca in mono version, but only in 1965. It comprised the hit single, one side of R&B covers, and boasted a second side of four songs written by Laine and Pinder. Later, Wharton left the management company, and this saw the group releasing a few singles deemed as "relatively unsuccessful." However, they enjoyed a small victory in the form of a cover of "I Don't Want to Go on Without You," which reached #33.

Later in the same year, a Pinder-Laine collaboration titled "From the Bottom of My Heart (I Love You)" was released as a single in May and performed slightly better. Sadly, another song penned by the duo, "Everyday," loitered at #44, and no other British singles were released for another year. On the upside, The Moody Blues lads were still very much in demand for live performances and had much success in the United States and Europe.

June 1966 saw Warwick depart from the group and the music world altogether. Rodney Clark succeeded him, but in October,

Clark also retired from the band. Clark's departure was a devastating blow, as it was announced he had joined The Rockin' Berries only a few days later.

Good news came in November 1966, when the re-formed Moodies made their appearance. With the success of the newly released single "Boulevard de la Madeleine," they won a sprinkle of new fans. This came just in time as the band was topping the Belgian charts and also relocated to the country for a stint. The change came about with new members Justin Hayward and John Lodge. Interestingly enough, Hayward came highly recommended by Burdon from The Animals.

After suffering financial losses and an altercation with an audience member, The Moody Blues realized that their way of covering American blues was no longer working. This saw them begin to focus on only producing their own material going forward. After an introduction to Tony Clarke from Decca, the band made "Fly Me High" and "Really Haven't Got the Time." Even though both songs failed to reach the charts in the United Kingdom, they still enjoyed good reviews and radio airplay. More importantly, the distinctive sound paved the way towards their musical evolution.

Enter the Mellotron. The world was first introduced to this new sound with the release of "Love and Beauty" and later with "Leave This Man Alone." The latter also failed to garner excitement in the United Kingdom but further solidified their new identity as a band.

When the band's contract with Decca Records was nearing the expiration date, they had already owed the label roughly £7,000 (US$9,192) in advances, and to make matters worse, the second album never came to pass either. But every cloud has a silver lining, and even with the financial issues and non-renewal of a Decca contract, the band was close to Hugh Mendl, and he signed them to a Decca subsidiary called Deram Records. They were offered a rock and roll remake of the song "New World Symphony," initially done by Antonín Dvořák. In exchange for the cover, all their debt with Decca was written off, and they could start on a proverbial clean slate. The band agreed to the terms with one condition: They were given artistic control. Mendl agreed to the terms, despite Decca's reservations. Unfortunately, the project was never finished and was abandoned in the end.

At first, Deram's executives had reservations about the intricate sound of the album. *The Days of Future Passed* (released in November 1967) was a concept album, which climbed to its summit at #27 on the UK LP chart. It would reach #3 on the US Billboard chart five years later. What makes a concept album or song cycle (LP) so great is that the entire creation is done over the course of just one day. As a result, this LP became a considerable source of inspiration for The Beatles. It just so happens that Pinder introduced them to the Mellotron, and they started to use this pioneering new technology as part of their repertoires.

The album was produced by Clarke, who was dubbed as "The Sixth Moodie," and he made both their singles and albums for the next 11 years. Derek Varnals (an engineer) also played a pivotal role in creating the Moodies' early studio sound. He worked closely with Clarke and Pinder to produce a more symphonic, overlapping sound on the Mellotron instead of the abrupt cut-off the device typically gives. This was done by removing any background sounds such as trains, whistles, etc. and then doubling up on the tapes with orchestral instruments.

Initially, the LP and two singles, "Nights in White Satin" and "Tuesday Afternoon," took time to appeal to audiences. The former only managed to peak at #19 on the British Singles Chart, and the latter didn't make the chart at all. However, later on, their native UK public started appreciating "Nights in White Satin."

After it was reissued, it managed to reach #9 in December 1972. Furthermore, it is nowadays classified as the signature Moody Blues song.

The next LP was released in 1968 and was titled *In Search of the Lost Chord*. There's a fascinating story about one song on the album in particular. "Legend of a Mind" was penned by Ray Thomas in tribute to one Timothy Leary (the LSD guru). Thomas performs a solo flute repertoire on the single, and it is said that the four members of The Moody Blues had experimented with LSD together at the beginning of 1967. The song's promotional film was recorded at the Groot-Bijgaarden Castle in Brussels, Belgium. After drawing inspiration from Beatle George Harrison, it was here that Hayward started practicing the sitar and incorporating it into the Moodies' music.

Fellow Moody, Graeme Edge, firmly secured his place in the band as a poetry writer. Some of their LPs in the late '60s actually comprise various band members reciting his poems, which Edge then turned into lyrics. Even though Edge wrote the lines and sonnets of his poem "Departure" on the Moodies' song "Lost Chord," he thought that Pinder had the better voice to recite it due to the raspy effect produced from his vocal cords as a result of drinking whiskey and indulging in many a cigarette.

The Moody Blues' sound became more symphonic and complex in nature throughout the next few years. It was laced with robust amounts of reverberation on the vocal singles, so much so that the release of the next album was inspired by the historic moon landing of Neil Armstrong and his crew and was titled *To Our Children's Children's Children*. The first single off the album, called "Higher and Higher," boasted a rocket blast-off-simulating sound produced by Pinder on keyboards.

The year 1969 brought about exciting new things for the band when they established their own record label, named "Threshold," under license from Decca Records. *To Our Children's Children's Children* was one of the first LPs released on their own label. By 1970, The Moody Blues had firmly cemented their place as a bill-topping musical act worldwide. That same year, a movie of their performance and the Isle of Wight Festival was released in conjunction with a new album. In the same year, it became known that Justin Hayward had been experimenting with a new guitar tone by using pedals and fuzzboxes—this added a beautiful, buzzing, melodic guitar-solo effect to the group's music.

The year 1971 saw another Moody music transformation when the band decided to go back to their roots by deploying an orchestral sound. This was both a blessing and a curse at the same time. Even though it was their signature sound, it was hard to recreate mid-concert. It's said that one single released in this year, titled "Every Good Boy Deserves Favour," was borrowed from a memory device called a mnemonic. This strategy is used by musicians to remember the notes that form the line of the treble clef: EGBDF. "Procession" was released as the opening track to the next album, also called *Every Good Boy Deserves Favour*. "Procession" became the only song penned by all five Moodies and tells the tale of the musical evolution to "Story in Your Eyes," written by Hayward. Pinder underwent a metamorphosis of his own when he started penning lyrics intended to be sung instead of his poems designed to be versed.

By the turn of 1972, two songs penned by Lodge, "Isn't Life Strange?" and "I'm Just a Singer (In a Rock and Roll Band)," were taken from the album *Seventh Sojourn* and subsequently became two charting UK singles in their own right. *Sojourn*, for short, saw Edge upgrade to an electronic drum kit and subsequently created the foundation for Pinder to use a Chamberlin instrument instead of the iconic Mellotron. By this time, other bands got interested in covering their songs. Some bands and artists who performed cover versions of Moody songs were the Four Tops ("A Simple Game," "So Deep Within You") and Elkie Brooks ("Nights in White Satin"). Pinder also got a very coveted invitation to appear on John Lennon's *Imagine* album and provided supporting percussion on the song "I Don't Wanna Be a Soldier (I Don't Want to Die)."

By the end of 1972, five years after the initial release, "Nights in White Satin" was awarded a re-issue and reached extraordinary new heights. It became the band's highest-ranking US single and peaked at #2 on the Billboard Hot 100, becoming a certified million-seller. The UK fans also started taking notice again, and the song was once again within the fold of the UK charts, topping at #9 (ten places higher than the original release).

In 1974, after touring most of Asia, the band decided to take a much-needed, long break. As with all families who spend excessive time together, Hayward cited in an interview that the band members were feeling exhausted, and some were overshadowed by others in the group. As a result of the interview, it was deemed a full-scale breakup. Each band member went in their own direction and focused on solo work and other personal endeavors.

Not to fret, as good news came in 1977 when it was announced that the band wanted to get back into the recording studio. They re-signed with old Decca Records label, and despite the band's reservations, a sloppy eight-song reunion album was slapped together. Decca stated their reasoning behind it was to create excitement by garnering public interest before the Moodies released a new album.

It appears that the contract reunion with Decca brought about a slew of misfortune in its wake. Not only did a fire break out in their recording studio, forcing an impromptu move to Pinder's home studio, but after the move, the literal forces of nature conspired to create the perfect storm, followed by torrential rains, flooding, and, ultimately, a landslide. And, to make matters worse, after much rivalry, division, and tensions were experienced, Pinder decided to quit the band before the new album recording was completed.

As if this wasn't enough (but wait, there's more!), Clarke also left, citing personal reasons, and Pinder later advised that he was not going to tour with the band as initially planned. The tensions within the Moodies and Decca only intensified after Clarke's revelation of super-high stresses and recoding room flare-ups with the rest of the band members. Decca, always wanting to save face, announced at a press conference that Mike Pinder was absent and currently in the United States, much to the dismay of the rest of the band. How catastrophic for rest the of band having two pivotal members quitting, and right after a comeback tour was announced to the entire music world!

Needless to say, the "Octave" World Tour still went ahead, and the Moodies were joined by Patrick Moraz from Yes for the season. The album produced many hits and enjoyed success globally. Throughout much of 1979, The Moody Blues were touring Europe and the United States. By 1980, the band was back in the recording studio bringing in Pip Williams as the producer. (Just a respectful side-note that Pip's fine musical creds include being a super-hot and in demand session guitarist, and also producing stelar acts like Graham Bonnet and no less than 10 of Status Quo's records, including their signature *Rockin' All Over the World* album – quite a hit; we'll get to Status Quo more in book 3 of the British Invasion series, the 70s bands). By the way, The Moody Blues decided to keep Moraz on permanently, much to Pinder's dismay.

This was not the only change that Moraz's presence brought into the fold. By this time, they had put the Mellotron and Chamberlin devices aside and focused on a more keyboard-rich sound instead. This meant that the band was moving away from the symphonic sounds to concentrate on a style boasting more of a contemporary edge. However, it bears saying that the Mellotron was still pulled out occasionally for live performances and even used in songs it was not previously included in during the recording process.

With their latest album release in 1986, *The Other Side of Life*, the band once again enjoyed renewed success and even received the Billboard Video of the year award for their song "In Your Wildest Dreams," after regularly featuring on MTV. By then, their new producers Visconti and Radman managed to produce a unique, contemporary sound that placed them in contention again with their pop genre counterparts. In the same year, the band was invited to play a four-song list for the Birmingham Heartbeat Charity Concert and would later provide backup support for ELO and George Harrison with their setlists.

Legal Disputes

In 1980, after Mike Pinder's hiatus from the "Octave" World Tour, he thought that he would be able to return to his regular spot and solidify his place as keyboardist. After the tour's success, the band chose to keep Patrick Moraz instead. Pinder said he was under the impression that he would be able to return to the band after the tour was completed. Needless to say, Pinder was less than pleased with the news that he wouldn't be joining again. He retaliated by taking legal action against the Moodies by preventing them from releasing the new album sans his contribution. However, he failed in his attempts and never returned to the band.

As fate would have it, the band later had troubles again in 1991, during the production of a new studio album. Mid-way, Moraz granted an interview with *Keyboard* magazine and aired his grievances with his role in The Moody Blues. He had a string of complaints, which included that their music's structure was too simple and that the other band members didn't play nice by not permitting him to make any significant songwriting contributions. Notably, he was spending more time planning a music concert in his home country of Switzerland instead of rehearsing with the band. This saw him being firmly Donald Trumped ("you're fired", as the saying goes) - sacked on the spot before the project saw the light of day. The Moodies also omitted to name him as a permanent band member and only credited him as an "additional keyboardist" in addition to cropping him out of album cover photos. This didn't sit well with Moraz, and he launched a lawsuit in the United States. He won, and the case even made it to Court TV. Initially, he sought $500,000 but was only rewarded with $77,175 as compensation in back pay.

During the rest of 1991 to 1992, the band had some album and singles successes and even did some highly-acclaimed live concert performances. It was also in 1991 that the band decided to take a break from recording and focus on live orchestral performances. The dry spell came to an end in 1999, but the album released in that year, called *Strange Times*, only enjoyed moderate success. This left Hayward tremendously deflated at the lackluster public interest. Hayward's swan song with the band came with "English Sunset" in the same year.

Some band members still performed live, toured, and recorded albums until 2018, when Hayward announced the band's disbandment after Edge retired in the same year. Our story comes full circle with The Moody Blues being inducted into the Rock and Roll Hall of Fame in Cleveland, Ohio on April 14, 2018.

The Band Legacy

The Moody Blues became pioneers by believing that a

successful rock and roll band can thrive as musicians under their own record label. Their label, Threshold, was formed with the idea in mind to make new albums and then send them off to Decca, who would act as their distribution partner. They aimed to develop new and emerging musical talent. They did manage to sign three bands called Trapeze, Providence, and even Portland, Oregon, but eventually, the idea fell flat, and they refocused on traditional recording contracts. But what can be said from this venture is that it created a foundation for other musical acts to establish their own labels and distribution channels. Some bands influenced by this include The Rolling Stones and Led Zeppelin.

Musical Influences

Their robust symphonic/art rock sound greatly influenced bands such as Genesis, Deep Purple, ELO, and Yes, to name but a few. In addition to that, they also played a big part in making synthesizers part of the rock scene.

The Moody Bluegrass

The Moody Bluegrass project, a group of Nashville musos, recorded two tribute albums of Moody Blues tunes in a genre known as the bluegrass style. The first album was released in 2004 and the second in 2011. During the first tribute album recording, the original Moody Blues members such as Edge, Hayward, Pinder, Lodge, and Thomas made guest performances.

Their Impact

The Moody Blues boys from the United Kingdom are considered one of the first progressive rock bands, and their music has had a significant impact on society. Their albums garnered much commercial success, and their music continues to be popular to this day.

Top Quotes from The Moody Blues

"When I came to The Moody Blues, we were a rhythm and blues band. I was lousy at rhythm and blues - I think the rest of us were." –Justin Hayward ("Justin Hayward Quotes," n.d.)

"We used to think that we were aiming at the head and the heart, rather than the groin. The Stones did (raunchy). You need balance. 'The Other Side of Life' was a try to get a really raunchy, dirty song, and it just didn't come out that way. We can't seem to make the crossover." –Graeme Edge ("Graeme Edge Quotations," n.d.)

Chapter 4
#7 - The Troggs

"That's a f***in' No.1! If that baaa-stard don't go, then oi'll f***in' retoire. Oi' f***in' do" –Ronnie Bond (drummer for The Troggs)

About:

D o you remember The Troggs? No, not the amphibians —the 1960s rock band. Chances are if you're a music lover of a certain age, you do. Even if you weren't born when they were popular, their songs have been covered so many times that you've probably heard one cover at least once in your lifetime.

Genre: Rock
Years Active: 1964–present

Discography:

The Troggs enjoyed a fruitful musical career and boast no less than 12 compilation albums, two live albums, nine studio albums, and 34 singles. What an amazing achievement! Some of their most memorable work includes the following:

Year	Album Name	Single Name	Chart Position
1966	*From Nowhere* (UK) *Wild Thing* (US)	"Wild Thing"	UK #2 US #1
1966	*Wild Thing* (US)	"With a Girl Like You"	UK #1
1966	*Love Is All Around* (US)	"I Can't Control Myself"	UK #2
1966	*Love Is All Around* (US)	"Anyway That You Want Me"	UK #2
1967	*Love Is All Around* (US)	"Give it to Me"	UK #12
1967	*Love Is All Around* (US)	"Night of the Long Grass"	UK #17
1967	*Cellophane* (UK) *Love Is All Around* (US)	"Love Is All Around"	UK #5 US #7

The Band Members

Member	Position	Years Active	D.O.B	From
Chris Britton	Backing vocals, lead guitar	1964–1969	January 21, 1944	Watford, Hertfordshire
Pete Staples	Backing vocals, bass guitar	1964–1969	May 3, 1944	Andover, Hampshire
Reg Presley	Lead vocals	1964–1969	June 12, 1941	Andover, Hampshire
Ronnie Bond	Drums	1964–1969	May 4, 1940	Andover, Hampshire
Toney Murray	Backing vocals, bass	1969	April 26, 1943	Dublin, Ireland

Artistic Facts

- Did you know that Reg Presley's initial career choice was that of a bricklayer?
- The song "Wild Thing" was written by James Wesley Taylor, a.k.a Chip Taylor. He is the brother of Jon Voight, the famous academy award nominated actor, and therefore he is the uncle of Angelina Jolie.
- Reg also wrote a book in the paranormal genre in 2002, and some people deem him somewhat of an expert on crop circles.
- Not specifically related to this band, but did you know that what is selected as the B-side of a single is dependent on the country in which it's being sold? This can change from country to country. Confusing for some – a treasure trove for others.
- When "Wild Thing" was released in 1966, Reg was still working part-time on a building site. After he heard the song being played on the radio, he hung up his overalls, divided his tools amongst his peers, and left the building industry permanently to pursue his dream of becoming a full-time musician.

Their Story

This is the group many people call the "first British punk band." Their story might be a short one in this book, but by no means does it imply it's any less impactful. Ronnie Bond and Reg Presley just happened to be childhood friends with big dreams. In the early '60s, they formed an R&B band in Andover, their home-town in the United Kingdom. In 1964, the two were joined by

Chris Britton and Pete Staples, and the name the Troglodytes, or Troggs for short, was born.

Their first stroke of luck came in 1965 when they were signed by The Kinks' manager, Larry Page, under Page One Records. Later, Page also lent them to CBS for their first single, "Lost Girl." Their claim to fame came with their Chip Taylor-penned song, "Wild Thing." It reached #2 in the United Kingdom and #1 in the United States in July of 1966.

This tongue-in-cheek song has a story of its own. It was in 1965 that a resident band run by famous actor Richard Burton's first ex-wife, Sybil, first recorded the song. It was on a trip to New York that Page first heard the demo. Page wanted to add "Wild Thing" to the B-side to make way for "Did You Ever Have to Make Up Your Mind?" The Troggs thought differently; they didn't like the harmonies in the song suggested by Page. On the recording day for "Wild Thing," the Larry Page Orchestra had been booked, and The Troggs were told to wait outside. With a quarter of an hour left on the clock, and just as the band thought they were out of luck, they were ushered inside the studio. All the forces of nature conspired that day. They had to carry their equipment inside, set up, tune up, record the songs, and then leave. Needless to say, magic happened! Both songs were recorded in less than 10 minutes!

"Wild Thing" boasted a simplistic, robust guitar riff with flirty lyrics that very soon became a staple at every hip shakin' garage party in the '60s. It is even more impressive that it was recorded on only the second take at the world-famous independent Olympic Studios in London (which has hosted recording sessions of many other famous artists like The Rolling Stones, Led Zeppelin, The Jimi Hendrix Experience, BB King, The Eagles, David Bowie, Pink Floyd and even The Beatles for one track!) and was masterminded by Keith Grant's engineering genius. Grant's amazing musical prowess engineered some 120 records which all made the top 20 in the UK and the US and included luminaries like Dusty Springfield's debut solo single, *I Only Want to be With You*, and Procul Harum's *Whiter Shade of Pale*. Grant's engineering can also be heard on many film scores of award winning motion pictures, such as *Cry Freedom*, *The English Patient*, *Shadowlands*, *The Italian Job*, *The Life Of Brian*, *The Fisher King*, *Jesus Christ Superstar* and *Shirley Valentine*. Back to "Wild Thing", interestingly enough, a dispute arose over the song's distribution rights in the United States, and it had to be released on two different labels (Atco and Fontana). At first, the band's success was pretty limited in America since they only started actually touring the country in 1968.

The band was indeed on a roll in 1966, and they produced a slew of other great hits. Among the most notable are "With a Girl Like You" and "I Can't Control Myself." The latter's release became their second and final dual-label release in the United States, and Fontana claimed the rights to all releases following suit. The year 1966 ended on a high for The Troggs with "Anyway That You Want Me" in December.

It was also a successful year in 1967 with the release of "Give It to Me," "Night of the Long Grass," "Love is All Around," and "Hi Hi Hazel." But unfortunately—all lucky streaks run dry at some point—the public's interest in the band started to fizzle out. Pete Staples was replaced with Tony Murray (from Plastic Penny) in 1969. And during their 1972–1973 tour, Britton was replaced by Richard Moore. By 1974, the band was desperate to recreate the success they'd experienced in the '60s, and after an underwhelming stint with Pye Records, they reunited with Larry Page, who was then in charge at Penny Farthing Records. What followed were two failed attempts. The first was a cover of the Beach Boys' single "Good Vibrations" and a reggae-inspired version of "Wild Thing." Then, after rejoining the band, Britton was again at odds with the band's schedule as he also started to manage a nightclub in Spain, and as a result, Colin Fletcher and Richard Moore had to take turns filling in for him during the recording of *The Troggs Tapes* album in 1976.

After the last album failed to really chart, they found a new home with New Rose (a French record label) in the '80s; under this label they released *Black Bottom* in 1982 and *Au* in 1990. Some relatively good news came again only in 1991 when they recorded *Athens Andover*. This was an 11-song collaboration between The Troggs and three members of the group R.E.M. The album was recorded in Georgia in the United States and released in March 1992. In an attempt to capitalize and ride the wave of musical reinvention, two new collaborations on "Wild Thing" were released. But it was only on the third attempt that they struck gold with a version of the song recorded with the character 'Wolf' (Michael van Wijk) from the UK TV wrestling sports show *Gladiators*. The song managed to peak at #69 on the UK Singles Chart. Presley received substantial royalties in 1994 when the band Wet Wet Wet produced a cover version of "Love Is All Around." It remained in the #1 spot for 15 weeks in the United Kingdom.

The Troggs were never out of controversy's reach, with many of their records being labeled as too suggestive to a younger audience, and some were even banned as a result. However, there's no denying that many years later, they are firmly in the mind of old and new audiences alike by enjoying a fanbase that is deemed as die-hard with the younger generation following suit.

Musical Influences

Many artists and bands have credited The Troggs with having a significant influence on them. Artists include Iggy Pop, Buzzcocks, and even The Ramones.

Their Impact

The Troggs' most famous songs all sold well over 1,000,000 copies, and each was rewarded with a gold disc. "Wild Thing" is listed as #257 on the *Rolling Stone* magazine's list of the "500 Greatest Songs of All Time." In addition to that prestigious accolade, they significantly influenced punk rock and garage rock.

The Troggs' music had a significant impact on society. Their raw, primal sound was unlike anything that had been heard before, and it struck a chord with people looking for something new and exciting. The Troggs' music appealed to teenagers and young adults looking to rebel against the status quo, and their songs became anthems for the counterculture movement.

In addition, The Troggs' music was embraced by rock critics and other musicians, and it helped to pave the way for the punk rock movement. As a result of their influence, The Troggs are often considered one of the most influential bands in rock history.

Wild Thing: The Story

Now, it seems that The Troggs weren't ones for a lot of talk, except for their lyrics. Their most famous song, "Wild Thing," has inspired many cover versions. Some of the notable music royalty that have belted out their rendition of the song include -

- Bruce Springsteen
- Jimi Hendrix
- Prince

- Fancy

US songwriter, Chip Taylor, is well-deserving of the credit in penning this song. Taylor received a call at 2 p.m. from music producer Gerry Granahan (A&R), who was looking for an original song for his new music protégés, Jordan Christopher and the Wild Ones. However, there was one catch: Taylor had to produce the song by the following morning! History was made. While the Wild Ones recorded a fine version of the song it has been totally eclipsed by the raunchy, energetic ride that The Troggs gave to the world.

Top Quotes about The Troggs and their version of Wild Thing

Granahan challenged Taylor on the phone to write a song immediately. Taylor picked up his guitar, and not long after, the first verse was written and ready. In an interview later, Taylor had this to say:

"What I had felt really good, but now I didn't know what the hell to say."

"I didn't know what the hell I was going to do for that second verse. My brain had gotten too involved in it, and I just didn't want to think about it anymore." (Shapiro, 2010).

Taylor had this to say about the versions that have been released of his song:

"I felt The Troggs captured the essence of the song,' Taylor says of Wild Thing. 'I loved what Hendrix did with it. Jimi took the song one step further with this really amazing, sweaty strum. The Senator Bobby version was a fun thing to do. I even thought the Sam Kinison version had a certain feel and energy to it. I liked what Prince and Warren Zevon did to it,' he continues. 'It's been great to

watch over the years as people have taken it in so many different directions.'"(Shapiro, 2010)

The Troggs are clearly much more than Wild Thing, but their super gutsy version of that masterful, riff-based song is the one we all remember, and other musos tip their hats to.

Chapter 5
#6 - The Yardbirds

I would say seeing the original Yardbirds with Jeff Beck and Jimmy Page at old Fillmore was a pretty powerful influence on me. – Ronnie Montrose (highly influential session guitarist and lead ax for the bands Montrose and Gamma)

About:

D o you remember that song "For Your Love" by The Yardbirds? Well, that band was pretty popular back in the day. But do you know who they really were? (Spoiler alert: they were a British rock band.) What I should also add is that many of the band members would later become musical champions in their own right in various top rock and roll bands.

Genre: Rock

Years Active: 1963–1968 and 1992–present

Discography:

Their story is an amazing one, spanning many amazing years, and they still continue to delight fans today. Amongst their eight original albums, 18 selected albums, two album appearances, three video albums, and 19 singles and EPS are the following:

Year	Album/Song Name	Chart Position
1965	"For Your Love"	UK #3 US #6
1965	*Five Live Yardbirds*	UK #5
1965	"Heart Full of Soul"	UK #2 US #9
1965	"Evil Hearted You"	UK #3
1966	*Yardbirds,* a.k.a *Roger the Engineer*	UK #20
1966	"I'm a Man"	US #17
1966	"Shapes of Things"	UK #3 US #11
1966	"Over Under Sideways Down"	UK #10 US #13

The Band Members

Members	Position	Years Active	D.O.B	From
Anthony Topham	Lead and rhythm guitar	1963	July 3, 1947	Southall, Middlesex
Chris Dreja	Bass guitar, backing vocals, rhythm guitar	1963–1968	November 11, 1945	Surbiton, UK
Eric Clapton	Lead guitar	1963–1965	March 30, 1945	Ripley, UK
Jeff Beck	Bass, lead, and rhythm guitar	1965–1966	June 24, 1944	Wallington
Jim McCarty	Drums, percussion, backing, and occasional lead vocals	1963–1968	June 1, 1945	Walton, Liverpool
Jimmy Page	Lead and rhythm guitar	1966–1968	January 9, 1944	Heston, Hounslow
Keith Relf	Harmonica, lead and rhythm guitar	1963–1968	March 22, 1943	Richmond
Paul Samwell–Smith	Bass, guitar, keyboards, percussion, vocals	1963–1966	May 8, 1943	London

Artistic Facts

- This band boasted no less than three of *Rolling Stone* magazine's five best guitarists of all time. This included Eric Clapton, Jimmy Page, and Jeff Beck.
- Jimmy Page later went on to form Led Zeppelin.
- In 1976, Keith Relf was electrocuted by his own guitar! It appears the instrument was not well-grounded at the time. He died while playing his beloved instrument in his home studio.

- Eric Clapton almost lost his life in 1981 due to alcohol abuse.

Their Story

The band was formed in the southwest suburbs of London in 1963. Later, Relf was joined by Topham, McCarty, and Dreja. The new band's first gig was in May 1963 at the Kingston Art School. After a few gigs in September, they changed their name from the Blue-Sounds to The Yardbirds.

The group got noticed first when they took over for The Rolling Stones as the houseband for the Crawdaddy Club in the United Kingdom. This saw them bursting on to the UK rhythm and blues scene.

In October, Topham quit the band and was replaced by Eric Clapton. It was also here that Giorgio Gomelsky became The Yardbirds' first manager and record producer. Under his guidance, the group toured Britain as a backup band for Sonny Boy Williamson II.

When their touring stint with Sonny Boy ended, the band signed to the EMI label in Columbia in February of 1964. They recorded more live tracks at London's Marquee Club on the 20th of March. The album that followed, *Five Live Yardbirds*, consisted mainly of American blues and rhythm and blues covers and was released nine months after recording concluded.

With Clapton in tow, the band recorded two blues singles, "Good Morning, School Girl" and "I Wish You Would." But it was only with the Graham Gouldman composition hit, titled "For Your Love," that the band scored their first win. The song boasted a powerful harpsichord solo by Brian Auger and managed to hit the #1 spot in the charts in Canada and the United Kingdom and peaked at #6 in the United States. However, the results were not what blues-purist Clapton envisioned. You see, he wanted more for the songs than three-minute singles delivered in rapid succession, sans full appreciation. This left Clapton feeling immensely frustrated, and he quit the band on March 25, 1965, only 24 hours before the single was due for release. By then, he'd had enough of the commercial bullshit to last him a lifetime. However, Clapton didn't leave on terms that were too bad, and he recommended to the rest that he be succeeded by a well-known and young session guitarist named Jimmy Page. After leaving The Yardbirds, Clapton joined John Mayall & the Bluesbreakers. Page, however, was very satisfied with his sessional work, which yielded a lucrative income source at the time. He was also concerned about his health and was bothered by the politics involved in Clapton's departure. Page accepted the offer and also recommended to The Yardbirds to give his good friend Jeff Beck a go. Beck made his Yardbirds debut a mere 48 hours after Clapton dropped the band. The highly influential Beck/Page dual-guitar lineup only lasted roughly a year, as you'll find in the following. It's all a bit complicated, but here's how it rolled.

In 1966, Beck's presence brought about a unique hammer-on, distortion, and fuzzy tone that fit right in there with the new style of beaty UK music. This saw the band explore the possibility of using eclectic arrangements similar to Gregorian chants, using the Asian and European techniques, with Beck infusing it with a strong influence from the Middle East (talk about a mouthful, 'eh?). In the same year, Jeff Beck was voted the #1 lead guitarist in the *Beat Instrumental* music magazine.

During Beck's stint with the group, they produced some pretty notable hit singles that included "Evil Hearted You," "Heart Full of Soul," "I'm a Man," "Shapes of Things," and "Over Under Sideways Down." The album *Roger the Engineer* was also produced in the Beck era. On the song "Heart Full of Soul," Beck's fuzzy guitar riff aided the band—and the United Kingdom, for that matter—to break into the Indian-influenced style. This saw them reach the UK Singles Chart sometime in 1965. Their follow-up track, "Evil Hearted You," was heavily laced with guitar reverbs, and the band could even be heard chanting in a Gregorian monk style. "I'm a Man" is also a hard blues-rock song incorporating the scratching guitar from Beck and shifting the tempo to combine Relf's harmonica to the max before going back to the original beat. This was another UK band first!

The band's first tour of America started in August 1965. Two albums were prepared for their US audience, titled *For Your Love* and *Having a Rave Up*. They were joined by the legendary Sam Phillips from Sun Studios in Memphis during the tour. He also produced the two songs in question. With Beck in tow, the band had three more tours of the United States and a quick hop to Europe in April of 1966.

When The Yardbirds released the single "Shapes of Things," the song was dubbed as the first classic out of the newly formed psychedelic rock era, and so with it, Britain entered the psychedelic scene. This happened a mere three months before The Beatles released "Paperback Writer." "Shapes," for short, was written by the band members themselves and peaked at #3 in the United Kingdom and #11 in the United States. It's said that Beck's feedback-focused guitar riff and Relf's anti-war protest lyrics became the band's personal embrace of the psychedelia craze.

The recording sessions for "Over Under Sideways Down" took place in April 1966, and with it, the album *Yardbirds* was born. The album was more commonly referred to as *Roger the Engineer* because this was written beneath a cartoon drawing by Dreja of The Yardbirds' then engineer Roger Cameron, and they also appeared on the album cover for the UK release of the record. A lesser-known fact is that the whole album was written by the band after the record company gave them a deadline of seven days. The result? A jam-packed mix of eclectic-sounding monk chants versus hard rock and tribal rhythms from the African continent. In the end, *Roger the Engineer* reached a coveted position on *Rolling Stones*' "500 of the Greatest Albums of All Time" (it reached #350). It was indeed a record-breaking album in so many different ways!

After the release of *Roger the Engineer* in 1966, Samwell-Smith called it quits after a drunken spell at Queen's College and became a record producer instead, leaving the band in a bit of a bind. So, Jimmy Page agreed to step into Samwell-Smith's shoes until Dreja had confidently got his "chops up" to jump into the role himself. This saw the band touring for a while with Page on bass and the duo of Dreja and Beck on guitars as they toured Paris, the United Kingdom, and the United States. With their last tour in California, Beck became ill and was rushed to a hospital in San Francisco. Now try to keep up here, as Page became the lead guitarist, and Dreja switched to bass guitar. The group's robust dual guitar attack came after Beck recuperated and reunited with them, with Dreja staying on as bass guitarist.

This powerful combination saw The Yardbirds creating the avant-garde-sounding "Happenings Ten Years Time Ago." John Paul Jones (future Led Zeppelin player) joined as bassist for this song instead of Dreja. Sadly, the lineup of Page-Beck did very little else from a studio perspective, except for "Great Shakes."

The band made great strides when they opened for both the super headliners of The Rolling Stones and the powerful combination of Tina and Ike Turner in 1966. Needless to say, Beck got fired in the end. There were multiple reasons behind his departure, including his utter lack of professionalism and hot-headed temper and Relf's constant drunkenness. After leaving the band, they caught up again with him towards the end of November. As it turns out, it would be revealed later that none of the aforementioned reasons had anything to do with Beck's departure. According to best sources, including Beck himself at the 1993 Rock and Roll Hall of Fame induction ceremony, he was fired, kicked out, sacked by the band for being too wound up, slightly erratic and, most telling of all, sometimes even deserting the band when they were on tour. His leaving the group was announced in the United States on the 30th of November. After the announcement, Beck continued to perform solo.

The first half of 1967 was spent touring the world and then performing a few shows in the United Kingdom before departing for North America. The Yardbirds' final album release came in the form of *Little Games* in July 1967 (only in the USA). The rest of the year was spent on tours throughout the United States with their new manager, Peter Grant. By then, their live shows were more experimental and heavier than before.

The band experienced heavy competition in the form of Cream and Jimi Hendrix, who were all very popular for their psychedelic, blues-rock sound. Even with this said, McCarty and Relf wanted to continue on the musical path inspired by classical and folk music. This brought them to loggerheads with Page, who wanted to continue playing heavy music (the kind that Led Zeppelin later became famous for). By the end of March, both McCarty and Relf left, but not after being asked to stay for one more tour of the United States.

In June of the same year, the band played their final shows and announced that McCarty and Relf were officially leaving. They returned to the United Kingdom and played their last concert in July. Late in 1968, Dreja and Page put together a new band where Grant acted as manager and Page as producer. Page announced that they would still be featuring the guitar, but this time with the addition of the Mellotron device. The exchange of hands continued in rapid succession. B.J. Wilson and Clem Cattini were earmarked as drummers, while Terry Reid was headhunted to replace Relf. Unfortunately, the timing wasn't right, and Reid declined due to a recording contract that was signed shortly before he was approached. He did, however, suggest Robert Plant. Robert Plant, in turn, recommended his friend John Bonham in the capacity of drummer. Later, Dreja became a rock photographer after leaving the group. This is where John Paul Jones stepped up to the plate and offered his services. They accepted and embarked on a tour of Scandinavia.

Finally, The Yardbirds were inducted into the Rock and Roll Hall of Fame in 1992 (note that the formal ceremony for their induction was actually in 1993). During the same year, Rock Artist Management approached Jim McCarty to chat about a possible Yardbirds reunion. This piqued Jim's interest, and his condition to acceptance was that he would do it only if Chris Dreja also came onboard. The management company contacted Dreja, and he agreed. The band's next gig was in conjunction at a London club with The Animals and was a complete hit. By then, The Yardbirds had John Idan for lead and bass vocals. They still have the very same management company today and occasionally work together.

The first reunion album was released in 2003, titled *Birdland*. The new lineup comprised Dreja, McCarty, Mayo, Idan, and Glen, with McCarty penning most of the new songs. Even ole' Jeff Beck came to the party by joining his former bandmates for "My Blind Life." Topham would also join the band for a one-night-only onstage appearance in 2005.

Bad news came towards the end of 2014 when McCarty announced to the world that The Yardbirds had disbanded. But in true Yardbirds style, the band came back with a bang a year later and has been touring occasionally since.

Legal Disputes

In January of '68, the band recorded their last official single prior to the band eventually morphing into Led Zep, released in March. Sadly, it didn't reach the Billboard Hot 100 chart by a mile! In March and April of the same year, they did a concert and recorded some album tracks while touring New York City. The band decided not to include the song "Knowing That I'm Losing You" on record and filed it away for a rainy day. However, when Led Zeppelin became successful, the record label Epic tried to release it. Let's just say after Page's lawyers filed an injunction, the entire album was quickly withdrawn from the shelves.

With the formation of "The New Yardbirds" soon after, the band appeared on promotional material on either one of the two known names. Then, in October 1968, it was announced that their Liverpool University appearance would be their last. It's widely speculated that the reason for this was a cease-and-desist order given to the band from Dreja, who cited that he still had power over the legal rights to anything relating to "The Yardbirds" name. This is where, officially, as of October 19, 1968, the band became known as Led Zeppelin. And this announcement meant the end of The Yardbirds as we know them... at least for the next 24 years.

The Band Legacy

This British group will forever be remembered for having the uncanny ability to convert R&B into rock. In addition, it will go down in history for being the band with not just one but three legendary guitarists.

The Yardbirds brought many innovations, including Page's use of a cello bow, the wah-wah pedal, and a distorted fuzzbox. Other notable innovations include a taped noise loop in live settings with an open-tuned guitar that promoted sitar sounds. In the end, it was this distinct sound that made them famous.

Their Impact

There's no denying that The Yardbirds were a significant part of the UK blues scene of the opulent and colorful '60s, with blues music reaching a wider audience and evolving into new and exciting forms. Their innovative guitar style and techniques (such as the "rave-up" breaks) lay the groundwork for the heavy metal and psychedelic rock movements as well as the punk rock and progressive rock genres. While playing extended instrumental improvs and textures, they had the uncanny ability to take these instrumental sections and elevate them into heavier sessions, influencing bands like Chicken Shack, who started playing a more aggressive style of music.

There are many in the music industry who would say that The Yardbirds were underappreciated, however, they remain a critical part of 60s music history and their influence can still be heard in many modern bands. Their songs remain very popular to this day.

Top Quotes from The Yardbirds

"Led Zeppelin didn't get that kind of Beatles screaming. We had a more sort of macho crowd. But I remember once in the early days of The Yardbirds, we were playing on an ice rink, and the stage was mobbed by screaming girls. I had my clothes torn off me. That's a really uncomfortable experience, let me tell you." –Jimmy Page.

"The Yardbirds came into the Crawdaddy Club a week after the

Stones finished their Sunday night residency. They had done it for almost a year, I think, and then we did it for a year. It was better when they were playing there because when they went, they took half the crowd with them, and it took us quite a while to build up our own following." –Eric Clapton ("Eric Clapton Quote," n.d.)

"After I saw Jimi (Hendrix) play, I just went home and wondered what the f*** I was going to do with my life." -Jeff Beck.

Chapter 6
#5 - Cream

The only band I was ever really into was Cream. And the only thing I really liked about them was their live stuff. 'Cause they'd play two verses, then go off and jam for 20 minutes, come back and do a chorus and end. And I love the live jam stuff; the improvisation. –
Eddie van Halen

About:

Cream was a highly popular band from the 1960s and the trio is considered one of the most influential rock bands of all time. Their unique sound and energetic performances set the stage for later rock bands such as Led Zeppelin and The Jimi Hendrix Experience. If you're a fan of classic rock, don't miss out on this incredible band!

Genre: Rock
Years Active: 1966–1968, 1993, and 2005

Discography:

With an amazing lineup, it's no wonder that this band made the top 10 list. Some of their eight albums, 13 compilation albums, and ten singles include the following:

Year	Album/Song Name	Chart Position
1966	*Fresh Cream*	UK #6 US #39
1966	"I Feel Free"	UK #11
1966	"Wrapping Paper"	UK #34
1967	"Strange Brew"	UK #17
1967	*Disraeli Gears*	UK #5 US #4
1968	"White Room"	UK #28 US #5
1968	"Anyone for Tennis"	UK #40 US #83
1968	"Sunshine of Your Love"	UK #25 US #6
1968	*Wheels of Fire*	UK #5 US #4
1969	*Goodbye*	UK #1 US #2
1969	"Crossroads"	US #17
1969	"Badge"	UK #18 US #65

The Band Members

Member	Position	Years Active	D.O.B	From
Ginger Baker	Backing vocals, drums, lead vocals, and percussion	1966–1968	August 19, 1939	Lewisham, London
Eric Clapton	Backing vocals, lead guitar, lead vocals, and rhythm guitar	1966–1968	March 30, 1945	Ripley, UK
Jack Bruce	Acoustic guitar, backing vocals, bass guitar, cello, harmonica, keyboards, lead vocals, and piano)	1966–1968	May 14, 1943	Bishopbriggs, UK

Artistic Facts

- It was somewhere during Clapton's stint with Cream and John Mayall's Bluesbreakers (1965-66) that the words "Clapton is God" began appearing on walls as graffiti all across England.
- One of the names that the trio wanted to call the band included "Sweet and Sour Rock and Roll." Eric suggested that they use "Cream" instead because, well, they were the best after all (especially with him in the lineup).
- Jack Bruce's full name is John Symon Asher Bruce.
- Towards the end of the band's lifespan, the trio used to stay in three different hotels and only get together a few minutes before the shows.

P. J. Chambers

Their Story

By mid '66, Clapton's reputation saw him being labeled as the most sought-after blues guitarist in the United Kingdom. By then, his career with The Yardbirds had concluded, and he felt Mayall's band was constricting his talents. Later that same year, he met Ginger Baker, who, together with Jack Bruce, was with the *Graham Bond Organisation* at the time. It seems that the trio met just at the right time as Baker had grown bored of Bond's mental instability copulated with his drug addictions. Let's just say the meeting between Clapton and Baker went really well. After Baker gave Clapton a lift home in his car, the two started chatting about how impressed Clapton was with Baker's driving. Baker responded that he wanted to have a tete-a-tete with Clapton as he had been thinking about starting a new band. Well, it just so happens that Clapton was thinking about it too!

Baker and Clapton had much admiration for the other's musical genius, and this saw Baker asking Clapton to come on board. By then, the band's name hadn't been established yet, but Clapton agreed nonetheless. However, it did come with one condition on Clapton's part, and this was that Bruce should join them. Apparently, the request was such a shock to Baker's system that he almost rolled the car off the road.

Bruce and Clapton first met when Bruce was playing for the *Bluesbreakers*. At the time, both were recording together for a group called Powerhouse. Clapton was so impressed with Bruce's singing and technical capabilities that he wanted to work with him regularly. Interestingly enough, when Bruce and Baker were in Graham Bond's group, they were known for constantly being at each other's throats violently. Call it somewhat childish, but they had on-stage fights and even went as far as fudging with each other's instruments before shows. Even after Baker fired Bruce from the band, he'd still arrive at shows. This irritated Baker so much that he threatened to cut Bruce's throat if he continued to rub him the wrong way. It must've been the Clapton magic, but Bruce and Baker shook hands, and Bruce joined Baker's new band. And this is when the name "Cream" was coined.

At first, the band was called "The Cream," but as soon as the first album was released, the "The" was dropped, and they began referring to themselves as just "Cream." The group's first (unofficial) debut occurred on July 29, 1966 at the Twisted Wheel. The official debut happened just 48 hours later when they were part of the lineup at the Sixth Annual Windsor Jazz & Blues Festival. At the time, they were still relatively unknown and did blues reworkings of hit songs, which the crowd absolutely loved. In October 1966, they also got a major increase in fans when they jammed with a recently arrived Jimi Hendrix. As it turns out, Hendrix was a fanboy of Clapton and was dying to play with him onstage. Very few people might know that Bruce was considered the band's primary vocalist in the early days, as Clapton was shy. It was only later that he earned his lead vocal stripes on songs such as "Badge," "Four Until Late," and "World of Pain," to name a few.

Cream's first album release, *Fresh Cream*, was recorded and released in 1966 and reached #6 in the United Kingdom and #39 in the United States. It was an intricate blend of blues covers and self-written band lyrics. One of the tracks on the album, "Toad," would go down in music history as one of the first instances of what we know today as "drum solo."

Cream's first visit to the United States occurred in March 1967 when they were booked for nine dates at New York City's RKO 58th Street Theatre. As with all things unknown, at first they didn't make a big impact there, and this saw them being placed at the bottom of a six-ensemble cast that all performed thrice on each of the nine evenings. Sadly, Murray the K (impre-

67

sario) later reduced them to only one song per date. After this sting, they returned to the United Kingdom in May to record *Disraeli Gears*, which became their second album release. It saw the light of day later in 1967 and reached the #5 spot in the United States and the United Kingdom. The album was produced by one Felix Pappalardi and Tom Dowd (engineer). Many people refer to the album as the band's entry into the American blues-psychedelic UK rock scene.

One song on the album, "Sunshine of Your Love," has a particularly interesting story behind it. Not only did it become the most popular song from the band and their unofficial band anthem, but its origins are also of interest to die-hard fans across the world. After a long, frustrating, and fruitless night at Bruce's apartment, he and Pete Brown somehow made magic happen with the rise of dawn. Brown gazed out of the apartment window at the now rising sun, and the words "It's getting near dawn" escaped his lips. A bleary-eyed Jack Bruce picked up his bass guitar and strummed out a riff. Brown started "feeling" Jack's double bass riff, and looking at Bruce, uttered, "When lights close their tired eyes." The rest, as they say, is music history!

With the now popular psychedelic drawings for the cover of *Disraeli Gears* (check it out here - https://en.wikipedia.org/wiki/Disraeli_Gears), the band moved the album's release back to make way for the new cover. Artist Martin Sharp's work was used, but this pushed the release back by several months. However, the wait was well worth it. The record is considered as one of the band's best efforts, a true masterpiece of Rock history.

Now set to take the United States by storm, Cream played two headlining gigs at the Fillmore and the Pinnacle respectively. The two concerts were deemed a great success, paving the way for their music to find a welcome home amongst the hippy (or hippie) generation. With their newfound fan-dom, the band started playing more extended sets that included impromptu jamming sessions, sometimes spanning as long as 20 minutes.

The band's third album, *Wheels of Fire*, was released in 1968 and was recorded in short studio sessions between July 1967 and June 1968. By then, still a relatively new concept, the release of a double album containing two LPs appeared to work for the extended solo work. *Wheels of Fire* also saw the band morphing from the blues scene towards a more semi-progressive rock genre containing many orchestral instruments. Recording work on the album concluded around June 1968. By then, the band members were exhausted from their hectic touring schedule and constant loud jam sessions and were thinking about calling it quits. In a 2016 interview with *Music Mart* magazine, the world would learn that both Clapton and Baker felt that at that point they'd had enough. Baker would go on to say that 1968 was a soul-destroying year for the three-piece ensemble. This was due to the increasing volume of Cream's songs. It didn't start like that, though. All three band members enjoyed their day jobs in 1966, and from there, the sound levels just went off the rails! In addition to this, Baker and Bruce reverted to their old bad habits of fighting, putting heavy strain on Clapton who was placed in the middle of the ever-feuding duo and had to play peacekeeper.

Another lesser-known reason is that Bob Dylan started piquing Clapton's interest. It all came about when the group now known as "the Band," released their debut record. This was like a breath of fresh air to Clapton. He had simply grown tired of Cream's music volume and their psychedelic sound. This made Clapton think of embarking on a totally different musical path.

After Cream's disbandment in July 1968, after mulling over it for almost 12 months, Baker and Clapton formed a new band, "Blind Faith." Clapton tried to employ the services of Steve Winwood, hoping that it would ease the tension between Baker and Bruce. In addition to this, Clapton also started his solo career, and this saw him performing with bands such as *Derek and the Dominos* and even *Delaney and Bonnie*. Bruce, in turn, also had a very successful solo career, and all three former Cream band members continued to play songs in their own capacity for the next 40 years.

Cream was inducted into the Rock and Roll Hall of Fame in 1993 and briefly reunited to perform at their induction ceremony. At first, the three weren't keen on performing together, but Robbie Robertson convinced them otherwise. The induction ceremony would be the first time the trio played together again after a 25-year hiatus. Apparently, the performance went so well that the band was considering going on a reunion tour, but as we know, this never materialized. Later, Baker and Bruce (both solo artists by then) briefly reunited and worked together in 1990.

Later, in May 2005, the group would reunite at Clapton's request for four nights at the same venue where they played their final concert in 1968, London's Royal Albert Hall. They never spoke publicly about these shows, as the band was sensitive to Baker and Bruce's health and the tragedy of their personal lives. Notably, the tickets for Cream's last four nights in question were sold out in less than 60 minutes after being released to the public.

The trio had so much fun that they performed three more nights for their US audience in October 2005 at Madison Square Garden. However, being the purist and perfectionist he was, Clapton later said that due to lack of rehearsal time and the resurfacing of old grievances, he felt their performance wasn't up to scratch.

During the 2006 Grammy Awards, Cream received a Lifetime Achievement Award to recognize their valued contribution towards modern music. Not long after the award ceremony, a DVD was released depicting the tale of their musical journey. In

April 2010, Bruce confirmed to the world that there'd never be another Cream concert, stating to the media that the band was no more. Sadly, Baker died in October 2019, after Bruce passed away in October 2014. This leaves Clapton as Cream's last surviving member.

The Band Legacy

With Bruce, Clapton, and Baker all coming from other successful bands, they are widely regarded as the world's first "supergroup." Bruce was the principal songwriter, with Baker and Clapton occasionally also penning lyrics. It's well-known by music circle members that Cream was one of the best bands out of the United Kingdom when it came to their proficiency with instruments.

Throughout their career, they've sold more than 15 million albums worldwide, firmly cementing their place among the ranks of the world's best musicians.

Their Impact

In the early 1960s, Cream's music was considered a radical departure from the norms of popular music. The band's heavy, blues-based sound and improvisational style were a hit with young people who were looking for something new. Cream's songs spoke to the frustrations and aspirations of a generation coming of age amid social and political turmoil.

The band's debut album, *Tainted Cream*, sold over 3 million copies and reached #1 on the charts. Cream's popularity continued to grow with each successive album, culminating in their performance at the Monterey Pop Festival in 1967. That concert was considered a watershed moment in popular music, and Cream's influence can be heard in the work of later bands like Led Zeppelin and The Rolling Stones.

Cream's music has stood the test of time and is still enjoyed by millions of fans worldwide. Their albums have been reissued multiple times, and they continue to be popular among both casual listeners and serious music fans. Cream's influence can be heard in modern rock, blues, and jazz bands, and their legacy is assured as one of the most important and influential bands of all time.

Top Quotes from Cream

"From the beginning, I knew intuitively that if nothing else, music was safe, and nobody could tell me anything about it. Music didn't need a middleman, whereas all the other things in school needed some kind of explanation." –Eric Clapton ("Quotes About Eric Clapton," 2019)

"When I was living in the States, Charlie came to see me at my house, and he said, 'I'd give you some tickets, but I know you would never go!' I won't go within 10 miles of a Rolling Stones gig. They're not good musicians, that's why. The best musician in the Stones is Charlie by a country mile." –Ginger Baker

"We never did all that onstage leaping about crap that all these other bands do... and we never will. We just played music." – Ginger Baker ("Ginger Baker Quotes," n.d.)

Chapter 7
#4 - The Kinks

I think when I was a kid, and I was in England and it was all about The Stones, The Who, The Kinks and The Beatles and that's what my dad was into. —Slash (from Guns 'N Roses)

About:

The Kinks were a popular music band in the 1960s and 1970s, known for their catchy tunes and witty lyrics. The Kinks were one of the first British Invasion bands to succeed in America with their song "You Really Got Me." The Kinks continued to produce hits throughout the 1960s and 1970s before disbanding in 1996. Despite their long absence from the music scene, The Kinks remain one of the most iconic British bands of all time.

Genre: Pop, rock

Years Active: 1963–1996

Discography:

Throughout The Kinks' illustrious career, they really gave some great songs that are still enjoyed on LP players to this day. Some of their 32 compilation albums, six live albums, 24 studio albums, and 78 singles include the following:

The British Invasion (the Bands) - The Best 60's Pop & Rock Music

Year	Album/Song Name	Chart Position
1964	*Kinks*	UK #3 US #29
1964	"All Day and All of the Night"	UK #2 US #7
1964	"You Really Got Me"	UK #1 US #7
1965	*Kinda Kinks*	UK #3 US #60
1965	*The Kink Kontroversy*	UK #9 US #95
1965	"Tired of Waiting for You"	UK #1 US #6
1965	"Set Me Free"	UK #9 US #23
1965	"Ev'rybody's Gonna Be Happy"	UK #17
1965	"See My Friends"	UK #10
1965	"Till the End of the Day"	UK #8
1966	*Face to Face*	UK #12
1966	"Sunny Afternoon"	UK #1 US #14
1966	"Dead End Street"	UK #5
1966	"Dedicated Follower of Fashion"	UK #12
1967	*Something Else by The Kinks*	UK #35
1967	"Dead End Street"	UK #2
1967	"Death of a Clown"	UK #3
1967	"Waterloo Sunset"	UK #2
1967	"Autumn Almanac"	UK #3

P. J. Chambers

Year	Album/Song Name	Chart Position
1968	*The Kinks Are the Village Green Preservation Society*	UK #47
1968	"Days"	UK #12

The Band Members

Member	Position	Years Active	D.O.B	From
Bobby Graham	Drums and percussion	1964–1965	March 11, 1944	Edmonton
Clem Cattini	Drums and percussion	1965	August 20, 1937	Stoke Newington, London
Dave Davies	Acoustic guitar, backing vocals, banjo, electric guitar, keyboard, lead vocals, lead guitar, piano, and slide guitar	1963	February 3, 1947	Fortis Green, London
John Dalton (Nobby)	Backing vocals, and bass guitar	1966 and 1969	July 7, 1941	St. Albans, Hertfordshire
Mick Avory	Drums, percussion	1963–1969	Unknown	Unknown
Nicky Hopkins	Keyboards, piano	1965–1968	February 24, 1944	Perivale
Peter Quaife	Backing vocals, and bass guitar	1963–1966 and 1966–1969	December 31, 1943	Tavistock
Rasa Davies	Backing vocals	1964–1968	Unknown	Fortis Green, London
Ray Davies	Acoustic guitar, backing vocals, electric guitar, harmonica, keyboards, piano, lead vocals, resonator guitar, and rhythm guitar	1963–1969	June 21, 1944	Fortis Green, London

Artistic Facts

- One of the Davies' brothers, Ray, had an affair with fellow muso, Chrissie Hynde, and they share a daughter.
- Did you know that the band name is derived from the word "kinky?" The group saw this in an episode of the TV show *The Avengers* and decided to shorten the name.
- Ray Davies suffered severe gunshot injuries in the leg in 2004. In New Orleans a mugger stole his wife's bag, and he chased in pursuit; he was shot and wounded in the process.
- One of the Davies' siblings (his oldest sister, Rene) died on Ray's 13th birthday. As if it wasn't sad enough that his birthday would forever be marked by sadness, Rene also gifted him his very first guitar—wait for it—on the day she died. It doesn't get more mysterious than that!
- At a certain point, Mick Avory almost joined forces with The Rolling Stones.
- Rod Stewart was briefly the lead vocalist for the Pete Quaife Quartet (more on this below).

Their Story

The two founding fathers of The Kinks were none other than the two Davies brothers born in the United Kingdom. Their parents passed a love of music in their genes on to the two boys. As a result, Dave and Ray played guitar, rock and roll, and even skiffle together. Later, the duo met Pete Quaife and his bud, John Start, while attending Fortismere School. Together, they formed the band "Pete Quaife Quartet." Their debut gig came in the form of a school dance; it was so well received that the band started jamming at bars and pubs in the area. The band had an impressive lineup of lead vocalists, which included none other than Rod Stewart. Rod left later to form his own band, Rod Stewart and the Moonrakers, who later became their local competition, so to speak.

In 1962, Ray Davies (the older of the two brothers) left to study at the Hornsey College of Art. Now the next part is a mouthful. While at college, Ray approached Alexis Korner, from the *Alexis Korner's Blues Incorporated* band, later that same year. He asked for some advice on how to get his act noticed. Alexis recommended Giorgio Gomelsky (former Yardbirds manager). Gomelsky put Ray in touch with *The Dave Hunt Band* (a group of musos who performed in the jazz and R&B hemisphere). The Pete Quaife Quartet (now known as the Ray Davies Quartet) supported Cyril Stapleton at a New Year's Eve Concert at the Lyceum Ballroom. While Ray was still with his own band, he joined the Dave Hunt Band ensemble. In February 1963, Ray parted ways with Dave Hunt to join the Hamilton King Band/Blues Messengers. After the spring term concluded, Ray left Hornsey College and joined the Central School of Art and Design. By this time, the Davies Quartet had changed its name again—this time to The Ramrods. To date, Ray will tell you that their most important gig was at the Hornsey Town Hall for their Valentine's Day concert.

By June 1963, the Hamilton King Band had disbanded, and The Ramrods continued to perform under various different names before settling on the title, The Ravens... well, for a short time at least! They got some notable figures to assist with scheduling their shows for the rest of the year. Some of these individuals included Larry Page, Shel Talmy, and even The Beatles promoter, Arthur Howes. They auditioned in vain for many record labels until 1964, when Talmy landed them a deal with Pye Records. Before signing with Pye, they had a new drummer in the form of Mickey

Willet. Sadly, Willet didn't last long, and Mick Avory succeeded him. Avory was quite a catch as he had already made a debut appearance with the then-unknown Rolling Stones.

During the same time, The Ravens decided they needed a new name that would serve as a permanent fixture going forward. Eventually, they settled on "The Kinks." Not only was it a new name, but the sexual innuendo attached to it would finally get them noticed. There are many fan theories out there, but one in particular details that Page said that the band's fashion sense had some kinkiness to it. To date, there is much speculation that Ray never really took a liking to the name... but hey, who are we to argue, right?

The band's first two singles, a cover version of "Long Tall Sally" and "You Still Want Me," failed to rank on the music charts. In fact, it was so dismal that Pye threatened to cancel their contract unless their third single would be successful. It was then that "You Really Got Me," penned by Ray, was produced. The song was recorded in June of '64 with a more polished feel. After that, Ray insisted on re-recording the song, but the record label refused. Ray, never one for throwing in the towel, was determined, and Talmy took the initiative to fund the process from his own pocket. Talmy approached IBC studio, booked the band, and re-recorded the song on take two on the 15th of July.

The single was released in the same year in August and accompanied by a television appearance and much pirate-radio coverage from the famous offshore pirate-radio ship. By August 15, 1964, the song entered the UK charts and peaked at #1 on the 19th of September. An American record label, Reprise Records, took notice and rushed to import the song after Mo Ostin signed The Kinks. After all was said and done, it also reached the Top 10 on the US charts. The song's signature gritty guitar riff became "their" sound. The solo piece on "You Really

Got Me" was played and produced by Dave. This was done using Dave's Elpico amplifier by cutting a lesion into the speaker cone. "You Really Got Me" was dubbed a significant influence on the American garage rock band movement and served as the pioneering song in the heavy metal and hard rock genres. After the song was released, most of the band's tracks were recorded for their first LP release, titled *Kinks*. The album was released in October of 1964 and boasted various covers and re-done traditional songs. Even more, this was after it managed to reach a coveted #4 spot on the UK charts. Three weeks after the debut record's release, The Kinks' fourth single, "All Day and All of the Night" (also penned by Ray), reached #2 in the United Kingdom.

The year 1965 was an interesting year for the band. The Kinks opened the year touring New Zealand and Australia with The Honeycombs and Manfred Mann. The rest of the year also brought tours with Mickey Finn and even The Yardbirds. Internal ructions started to rear their ugly heads between the band members. One such incident was the very public and on-stage debacle between Dave and Avory while performing at the Capitol Theater in Wales in May. Notably, the argument escalated quickly when it got physical after only one song was performed. Pun intended, but it seems that Dave and Avory really got each other... meaning under the skin! Dave proceeded to verbally insult Avory and even kicked over his much-treasured drum kit. Avory, never one to walk away from a fight, smacked Dave in the head with a hi-hat stand. Dave passed out on the floor, giving Avory such a big fright (he thought he killed Dave) that he fled the scene with his tail between his legs. Dave was rushed to the Cardiff Royal Infirmary, receiving 16 cranial stitches. To make matters worse, when the constabulary arrived, Avory lied to them to avoid persecution and told them that it was all part of the band's new act, whereby flinging instruments at one another was the primary action.

After touring the United States in the third quarter of 1965, the American Federation of Musicians refused to furnish the band with the required permits for the next four years. Sadly, just as The Kinks entered the peak of the British Invasion, they were cut off from its folds and their income. Seems like we'll never know the reason why because the association nor the band ever revealed it. However, as the rumor mill goes, it's said that it was attributed to their then-recent animalistic antics on-stage (a.k.a, the hurling of instruments and the fighting). Others speculate that the actual ban came after the taping of the 1965 show *Where the Action Is*. Ray said an unknown dude randomly approached The Kinks from the TV network who accused them of being late. Apparently, it didn't stop there, and the same guy started making some very anti-British comments to them. One of the things being said was something about The Beatles being a hit, and The Kinks think they can do the same with their acne faces. So what followed? A good 'ole punch was delivered to the said perpetrator. And this, friends, is what brought about the ban, apparently. Guess we'll never know the truth.

The band made history en route while busy with their tours of Asia and Australia, respectively. Ray wrote the song "See My Friends," which was released in July of '65 as a single. This is one of the earliest examples of what we've come to know as "crossover music." In addition, it was one of the world's first pop-genre songs from the '60s to embrace and promote the influence of Indian music from the continent. Ray penned the song after taking a stroll and hearing the local fisherpeople chant. Let's just say it got the creative juices flowing! Interestingly enough, Jonathan Bellman, a music historian, thinks that "See My Friends" had a significant influence on other songwriters of the time. He feels that The

Beatles are receiving high acclaim for their song "Norwegian Wood" for the use of its sitar sounds. But, interestingly enough, The Beatles' song was released well after The Kinks' song saw the light of day.

This claim from Bellman can be further substantiated by a statement released by Barry Fantoni. Fantoni was a celebrity in his own right and a friend of the stars. He could count notable bands such as The Who, The Kinks, and The Beatles in his friend arsenal. Now, Fantoni also claims that he was visiting The Beatles, and they all sat around the gramophone and heard "See My Friends." It was then that The Beatles insisted that a sitar be added to their music montage.

Unfortunately for the band, the US audience despised their new sound, even after the song hit #10 in their home country of the United Kingdom. It only managed to reach #111 in the United States. This saw The Kinks springing into action to record *Kinda Kinks* the day after returning from Asia. What followed two weeks later was a new LP where 10 of the songs released were originals. Ray later said they weren't entirely happy with the versions released but had no choice due to pressure from their label. Later, also in 1965, the act's most notable stylistic shift became apparent with the release of two new singles ("A Well Respected Man" and "Dedicated Follower of Fashion") and a third album (*The Kink Kontroversy*). With the new album, Nicky Hopkins made his debut appearance on keyboards.

In the summer of 1966, the song "Sunny Afternoon" was released. It was especially good because it knocked "Paperback Writer" (Beatles) right off the #1 spot. Due to all the internal squabbles and extensive tour dates, Ray suffered a major physical and nervous breakdown and took an extended hiatus. During his recovery time, he had ample opportunity to reevaluate the band's direction and pen a few new songs. During the same time, bassist Quaife got injured in a car accident, and shortly after he recovered, he announced his departure from The Kinks. At the time, John Dalton was hired as a proxy while Quaife was recovering. After Quaife's departure, Dalton was officially hired as his replacement. It didn't take Quaife long to regret his decision, and he rejoined the group. Sadly, this meant that Dalton was out of luck, and he went back to his day job as a coalman.

The next single, "Waterloo Sunset," was released around May 1967. Now, there is a fascinating fan theory around the song. It's rumored that the song was inspired by the love affair between actors Julie Christie and Terence Stamp. The song lyrics depict two star-crossed lovers walking over a bridge near Waterloo Station while a melancholic third party looks at them, the Waterloo station, and the Thames River. Ray busted this fan theory in 2008, where he claims that the song was about a fantasy he had where one of his sisters emigrated to another country and how sad he would be if she left. Even for its complex arrangement, the song only took 10 hours to record. Ray later said that The Kinks spent quite some time developing a unique guitar sound.

The band then decided to use the tape-delay echo method, which hadn't been used since the '50s. This technique is the signature sound of Hank Marvin from the famed Cliff Richard and the Shadows. Why is this significant? Because, at the time, John Lennon said that in his opinion it was the only good thing that had come from the United Kingdom in the late '50s music scene.

Even though it wasn't new, the novelty was immediately noticed by Steve Marriott of The Small Faces, and he asked Ray how they'd achieved it. As it turns out, "Waterloo Sunset" would receive wide acclaim. Not only did it reach #2 on the UK Melody Maker's chart, but it also became one of their most-loved songs. Furthermore, 45 years after its release, it was chosen as the closing song of the 2012 London Olympic Games; it leaves one with goosebumps, doesn't it?

The single "Autumn Almanac" was released in October 1967 and reached a coveted #5 spot on the UK charts. Later, Andy Miller would rain on the band's parade by stating that it would be the group's last Top Ten UK entry for the next three years. Some say it was also the start of trouble for the ensemble. Towards the end of the year, it started becoming all the more evident that The Kinks were beginning to go out of fashion (and out of favor with the crowds).

In early 1968, the band mostly retired from touring and turned to studio work. Unfortunately, due to the band's unavailability to promote their material, the releases weren't met with much enthusiasm. In the wake of the bands waning popularity, Ray continued to focus on his own songwriting endeavors, but due to increased demands, The Kinks continued their studio work. After not much further success, the band released "Days." What would follow was a quick flash comeback and a single reaching the UK #12 spot but failing to chart in the United States.

By the start of 1969, Quaife again expressed interest in leaving The Kinks. The band thought it was a joke at first—until they saw an article with Quaife's picture attached to a new band, "Maple Oak." As it turns out, he was already performing with this new group without letting Ray or the others know. Ray begged Quaife to stay with the band until the recording sessions of the upcoming album were complete, but he refused. Ray turned to John Dalton and asked him to replace Quaife. Dalton agreed and stayed with the group until 1976.

In April 1969, Ray traveled to the United States to negotiate an end to their music ban. The negotiation was successful, and the management had to make travel plans quickly. Before returning to the United States, the group recorded "Arthur (Or the Decline and Fall of the British Empire)." It was deemed a modest success but was well received by US critics. The act departed for their US tour in October of 1969 but was largely unsuccessful, resulting in the majority of the tour dates being canned.

In May 1970, John Gosling joined the band, and the single "Lola" was recorded. The song had a very delightful (and a not-so-delightful outcome). The cheeky piece depicted the story of a male virgin who became "confused" after a romantic encounter with a transvestite. The song became a UK and US Top 10 hit, restoring them to good public favor. Notably, the song's original lyrics had the word "Coca-Cola" in it, and this saw the BBC refuse to give the song airtime. It bears understanding that the BBC had a strict policy governing the use of product placement in music at the time. So, in other words, artists weren't permitted to use the name of a product in their songs. Irritated, Ray agreed that the piece be re-recorded, and the line changed to "cherry cola" instead. But in true Kinks' fashion, the Coca-Cola version was still being used long after the debacle.

After the group's contract expired with Pyre and Reprise, they managed to sign a new five-record deal with RCA before the clock ran out in 1971. As part of the deal, the Kinks received a $1,000,000 advance, which they put towards constructing their own recording studio, affectionately called "Konk."

In 1972, a double album was released. One song in particular, "Celluloid Heroes," told the sad tale of the reflection on life had one been a movie star instead of an average Joe. The album reached #47 in Record World's chart and #70 on the Billboard Hot 100. The record is also significant because it served as the band's transformative years into the '70s music scene, a place where they firmly remained for the next four years.

In 1973, the band started incorporating female backup singers and added the horn to their musical instruments. Unfortunately,

Ray's marriage went to the dogs during this period, and the missus and kids left him. After that, he ultimately reached rock bottom. He was so over it that he declared on-stage to an audience that he was apparently just f***ing tired of the whole thing. Later, he would be rushed to the hospital for a drug overdose. Plans were hastily made for Dave to take his place if need be. Even though Ray made a full recovery, it was evident with the band's declining popularity that Ray and The Kinks would never be the same again.

After the band's contract termination with RCA, they signed a new deal in 1976 with Arista Records. This saw them transitioning to the rock genre after Dalton left the band. The release of their single "Sleepwalker" in 1977 earmarked the return of The Kinks as a younger generation have come to know and love them.

In the third quarter of 1983, the band released *State of Confusion*. At the same time, Ray started working on a solo film project, which caused a lot of tension with the other band members. Ray directed, wrote, and produced the movie *Return to Waterloo*. The synopsis details a London commuter who has a serial killer fantasy. It seems this solo project was the catalyst of many problems for the band. Not only did Ray and Chrissie Hynde's affair come to an end, but bitter archrivals Dave and Avory were at it again (funny, not funny). The feud got so intense that Dave refused to work with Avory. Eventually, Ray had no choice but to replace him with Henrit, and Avory was offered the role of studio manager for Konk, which he eagerly accepted.

In 1986, the band signed two deals: one with MCA Records in the States and one with London Records in the United Kingdom. Their first album with the labels, *Think Visual*, was released later the same year and managed to peak at #81 on the US charts. In 1990, they first became eligible for entry into the Rock and Roll

Hall of Fame. Avory and Quaife were on hand for the ceremony; however, by no means did it reboot their musical careers.

In 1990, the Britpop boom was experienced, once again placing The Kinks on the map. This was mainly due to the majority of the influential bands of the time crediting The Kinks as their musical influence.

In mid-1996, the band gave their last public gig, and later that year, they decided to reunite for one last time at Dave's 50th birthday bash. The party was held at the Clissold Arms pub—a new business venture for the Davies brothers. It was made all the more bittersweet because the pub was located right across the street from the childhood home where the boys grew up and jammed together for the first time. The Davies brothers did indeed come full circle.

The Band Legacy

This group is widely regarded as one of the most prominent rock genre acts out of the '60s, and this saw them ranked at #65 on *Rolling Stone* magazine's "100 Greatest Artists of All Time" list.

The band also has two records on *Rolling Stone* magazine's "500 Greatest Albums of All Time" list. They are *The Kinks are the Village Green Preservation Society* and *Something Else by The Kinks*.

Finally, they also have three songs on the same magazine's "500 Greatest Songs of All Time" list as of September 2021. The songs are

- "Waterloo Sunset" - #14
- "You Really Got Me" - #176
- "Lola" - #386

Musical Influences

The Kinks have influenced many punk rock acts like Blondie and The Jam. In addition, some heavy metal groups have also credited them as the inspiration behind their sound. Some of these acts include Van Halen and Pulp.

Craig Nicholls (The Vines) even said at one point that The Kinks' songwriting abilities have been heavily underrated. The Who's Pete Townshend also paid Ray Davies, in particular, a significant compliment. He stated that Davies influenced his pop writing lyrics from the very start.

Some other notable Kinks' influences include

- Joe Harrington: said that the band helped Jerry Lee Lewis transition from rock and roll to rock.
- Brian May (Queen): credited the band for pioneering the use of guitar riff music.

Their Impact

The Kinks were one of the greatest rock bands of the 60s British Invasion, and their music had a profound impact on society. Their songs were filled with biting social commentary, and they challenged the conventions of popular music. They helped pave the way for the punk movement, and their music continues to be influential today.

Thanks to The Kinks, young and old music lovers are opened up to a greater understanding of the complexities of human relationships and the challenges of everyday life. They showed us that it is possible to be creative and innovative while still maintaining a sense of social responsibility. They continue to inspire new generations of musicians and artists. The Kinks are a vital part of musical history, and their music will never be forgotten.

Top Quotes from The Kinks

"We've always had our hardcore fans. But the general public has a love-hate thing about the 'Kinks.' It always leaves people with a question mark on their heads." –Dave Davies

"Working with the Kinks, there always seemed to be some kind of automatic process at work. Ray and I had this telepathy happening for a long time, where one of us always knew what the other could do with something." –Dave Davies

"Ray is very secretive about his ideas - why not, the times that the Kinks have been ripped off, especially in the early years, it makes you a little bit cautious about telling anybody what you're doing. And that's understandable." –Dave Davies ("Dave Davies Quotes," n.d.)

Chapter 8
#3 - The Who

It was pretty radical (for me) to go from the Eagles to being the only melodic instrument (in a band). You have to play a certain way. It's like the Who. It was a great kick in the pants for me to get my chops up and to improvise a little more. –Joe Walsh (from the Eagles, and Ringo Starr and His All-Star Band)

About:

Who were The Who? They were an on-again, off-again British rock band that formed in 1964. They became famous for their live performances and hits like "My Generation" and "Won't Get Fooled Again." But there's more to The Who than just their music.

Genre: Blues, rock

Years Active: 1964–1983, 1985, 1988–1991, 1996–1997, and 1999–present

1960's Discography:

These London boys had much success during their career. Their music was truly one for the books. Some of their 32 compilation albums, 16 live albums, 14 studio albums, and 58 singles include the following:

Year	Album/Song Name	Chart Position
1965	*My Generation*	UK #5
1965	"I Can't Explain"	UK #8
1966	*A Quick One*	UK #4
1966	"Happy Jack"	US #27
1966	"I'm a Boy"	UK #2
1967	*The Who Sell Out*	UK #13 US #17
1968	"Magic Bus"	UK #25 US #26
1969	*Tommy*	UK #2 US #1

The Band Members

Member	Position	Years Active	D.O.B	From
Doug Sandom	Drums	1964	February 16, 1930	Greenford
John Entwistle	Backing vocals, bass guitar, horns, lead vocals	1964–1969	October 9, 1944	Chiswick, London
Keith Moon	Backing vocals, drums, lead vocals	1964–1969	August 23, 1946	Wembley
Pete Townshend	Backing vocals, keyboards, lead guitar, lead vocals, rhythm guitar	1964–1969	May 19, 1945	Chiswick, London
Roger Daltrey	Backing vocals, harmonica, lead vocals, rhythm guitar, and percussion)	1964–1969	March 1, 1944	London

Artistic Facts

- The Who was the first musical act to successfully produce a rock opera in 1969.
- On May 31, 1976, the band broke the Guinness Book of World Records for the world's loudest music concert several times in one day. They received the accolade for the world's loudest music concert. After try number seven, the auditing committee asked them to stop because people were losing their hearing (that's how loud it was).
- Thunderfingers was one of the nicknames his bandmates gave Entwistle.

- Daltrey is the only band member not to get involved in drugs. His curiosity only went as far as experimenting with marijuana.
- Daltrey is also the only band member who has been in a stable marriage with his wife since 1971.
- In February of 2010, The Who got a lot of screen time when they performed at the Superbowl XLIV, in Florida, for the halftime show.
- The song "Who Are You" is used as the theme song of the hit US TV show *CSI-Miami* (yes, the one with the dude with the red hair and the intense stare and cool shades).

Their Story

The three founding members of The Who—Daltrey, Entwistle, and Townshend—all grew up in London and all attended Acton County Grammar School. Townshend's parents both performed for the Royal Air Force entertainment division during WWII and firmly supported their son's rock and roll endeavors. Townshend and Entwistle formed a traditional jazz band during their school years.

At the time, both Entwistle and Townshend had a keen interest in rock and loved Cliff Richard's single "Move It." Unable to afford a bass guitar and having issues with a standard guitar, Entwistle built a custom piece at home. After finishing school, Townshend went on to attend Ealing Art College.

Daltrey, on the other hand, was a year older than the other members, and his parents moved from Shepherd's Bush to Acton. Daltrey found it challenging to fit into the new worker's class, but salvation later came when he discovered rock and roll... and gangs! He was expelled from school and sought work at a construction site. In 1959, he formed the Detours (later called The Who). The group played at corporate gigs and weddings, and Daltrey was responsible for the act's music and financial affairs.

How Daltrey and Entwistle met up after finishing school was entirely by chance. Daltrey saw him walking on the street, carrying his custom guitar, and after a quick chat, he invited Entwistle to join the Detours. In the third quarter of 1961, Entwistle recommended asking Townshend onboard as a guitarist. The Detours played trad jazz and pop covers with Colin Dawson on vocals, Jackie Wilson on drums, Daltrey on lead guitar, Entwistle on bass, and Townshend on guitar. As these things go, Dawson withdrew from the band, as he and Daltrey never seemed to agree on anything concerning the band. After Gabby Connolly replaced Dawson, he moved to lead vocals, and Townshend to the only guitarist.

Pete Townshend's mum got the band's first contract with a local promoter, and he started booking them at performances as a supporting act. Today, The Who credits bands such as Shane Fenton and the Fentones and Johnny Kidd and the Pirates as their musical influences during their formative years. Townshend, in particular, was very fond of how the Pirates' sole guitarist, Mick Green, used a combination of lead and rhythm guitar in their music style. This also inspired the band to transform Entwistle's role into a lead instrument that produced melodies. The name change occurred in February 1964 when Townshend sat across from his flatmate Richard Barnes and played around with new band names. Townshend wanted something jokey. Among the names penned down was "The Hair" and "The Who." Pete presented his findings to Daltrey the following day, and the name "The Who" was born.

By the time the new permanent name change was in place, the group had played regular gigs and replaced their first manager with Helmut Gorden. The band auditioned for Fontana records and impresario Parmeinter. Parmeinter was not happy with the drumming and voiced his concern to Townshend. Townshend, annoyed with Doug Sandom (on drums at the time), threatened to fire him if his playing didn't drastically improve. Sandom didn't take lightly to threats and decided to leave. However, he didn't part ways with The Who before Townshend called in a favor (cheeky much?). Townshend convinced Sandom to lend his drum kit to any replacement band members or session drummers The Who had to use. It turns out Townshend and Sandom didn't speak again for 14 years after the incident.

It was during a performance at the Oldfield that The Who got acquainted with Keith Moon. Keith had been playing drums in bands since 1961. Moon was playing semi-professionally for the Beachcombers when he met The Who and was seeking a full-time gig. The Who asked Keith to do an audition for them. The result? He tore a drum skin and broke a bass drum pedal in the process. After Moon's jaw-droppingly good performance, Townshend hired him on the spot. Moon still stayed with the Beachcombers for a while, but it got increasingly difficult to play for both bands. In the end, he chose to devote himself to The Who.

Very few people might know that even after the permanent name The Who was chosen, they were briefly called the High Numbers. This came at the insistence of their new manager, Peter Meaden. Meaden believed that if the band's name changed, along with their fashion, look and style as well as their sound, they would be more successful. Meaden secured them a second audition with Fontana Records, who signed them this time around. Meaden then went on to pen "Zoot Suit," the band's first single. After the single failed to make the top 50, the band said 'screw it' and changed the name back to The Who.

After the name was changed back, it seems that The Who

started improving their on-stage presence as well. This all seemed to come like second nature since none of the band members played their instruments in a traditional manner. Daltrey started using his mic cable like a whip and frequently jumped into the crowd. Moon showed off his drumstick tossing talents mid-beat, and Townshend pretended to machine-gun the crowd with this guitar. Simultaneously, Townshend's now-famous pose "the Bird Man" became a thing. It involved Townshend standing aloft with his arms spun out wide and striking across the strings, which in turn produced amp feedback.

In June 1964, after replacing Meadon with Lambert and Stamp (two filmmakers), the band started working on a promotional film. It all started with the two filmmakers seeking a relatively unknown band to make a movie about. During one of their regular performances, Townshend got chatting to Lambert, and the idea was born. For the film, the band focused on motown covers, rhythm and blues, and soul. The slogan "Maximum R&B" was also coined on the same day. It was this performance, in particular, that got them noticed big time! While mid-set, Townshend broke the head of his guitar by mistake after knocking it on the stage ceiling. Townshend got so upset with the now laughing crowd that he completely smashed it to smithereens on stage. What happened next? He picked up another guitar and continued with the set. Townshend's act became so popular that the audience requested to see something similar the next time they played at Railway. After a carefully planned act, Moon kicked his drum kit over, and what followed was a phrase called "auto-destructive art." Let's just say after that, their instrument-killing endeavors formed part of every performance.

The release of the feature film came late in 1964 and similarly also got the attention of The Kinks' producer Shel Talmy. In response, Townshend wrote the song "I Can't Explain." You see,

Townshend penned the song to sound just like a song The Kinks would sing, and in turn, this saw Talmy sign them to his production company. The song became very popular with pirate radio stations and received a lot of air-time. The significance of this is that pirate radio was very important for groups in the pop genre. At the time, there were no commercial radio stations in the United Kingdom, and then, BBC Radio seldom played pop music. The song slowly climbed the charts and, in early 1965, made a turn in the Top 10.

Their next single, titled "Anyway, Anyhow, Anywhere," was written by Daltrey and Townshend. The song was very unconventional and unique, so much so that it was rejected at first by Decca Records in the United States. The song boasted special guitar sounds such as feedback, pick sliding, and toggle switching. Notably, the song was so popular in the United Kingdom (after reaching the Top 10) that the TV show *Ready, Steady Go!* adopted it as their theme song.

After a disagreement between Daltrey and Lambert and a failed R&B cover recording session, it really started going to the dogs. As it turns out, the only group members that really got along were Entwistle and Moon. Things came to a boiling point when the band toured Denmark in September. Daltrey proceeded to flush Moon's amphetamines down the toilet and threw a few punches at the drummer. None of this sat well with the band, which fired Daltrey when they returned home. Later, he was reinstated, with the condition that, going forward, The Who would take matters to a vote when needed instead of suffering under Daltrey's dictatorship.

In October, the group's next single, "My Generation," was released. Initially intended as a slow blues tune, it was transformed into a powerful tune with the help of Entwistle's bass solo. Other gimmicks in the song included vocal stutter and key changes. The single became the group's highest-charting song in the United Kingdom.

Throughout 1966, the band's feuds with one another continued. After appearing on *Ready, Steady Go!* with Bruce Johnston (The Beach Boys), Entwistle and Moon arrived late at a gig. Townshend got very upset and smashed his guitar in Moon's face. Moon had a black eye and some other bruises (including his ego). Being fed up with the whole affair, Moon and Entwistle quit the band. It wasn't long after that they changed their minds and went back.

In August 1968, The Who performed at Woodstock. They were very reluctant to perform and demanded an upfront payment of US$13,000 to appear. Initially scheduled to play on the 16th of August, the festival ran late, and the band only started playing at 5 a.m. on the 17th. During their set, they played most of the singles from the album *Tommy* (about a deaf and blind boy navigating through life). After such a long on-stage delay, "Yippie" (Youth International Party) leader Abbie Hoffman went on stage mid-set and gave a impassioned speech about political activist and jazz poet, John Sinclair. Townshend was extremely upset at Hoffman, and he was kicked off stage, but not before Townshend shouted a few profanities at him. The band's set ended just as the sun started rising, which saw Townshend throwing his guitar into the audience. Even though the band received wide acclaim for their Woodstock performance, they hated every minute of it.

The movie of the album *Tommy* made history for the band and also made them a lot of money in the process. This saw each band member reacting in different ways towards their newfound wealth. Entwistle and Daltrey lived lives of comfort. Townshend felt embarrassed because the money he was earning was at odds with his new religion (Meher Baba) and its teachings. And Moon, well, he was a big spender!

The band eventually went back to touring, and singles "Baba

O' Riley" and "Won't Get Fooled Again" became live crowd-pleasers. While on tour in December 1971 at the Civic Auditorium in the United States, Moon passed out mid-set. It turns out that he overdosed on barbiturates and brandy. After a quick break, he was back and completed the performance as if nothing had happened.

Who Are You was released in August of 1978, but with it came sad news. Not only had the band needed to replace Moon on a song, but he had become very ill. Even though the album later became the band's fastest and biggest-selling record to date, it was tainted with sadness. After the band attended a party, Moon took 32 tablets of clomethiazole, passed out, and was found dead a day later.

The band continues to perform to this day, much to the delight of their die-hard fans!

The Band Legacy

The band has been categorized as one of the most influential rock ensembles of the 20th century—and still holds sway in the 21st century! Their legendary appearances at places like Woodstock and Monterey have firmly cemented their place in music history as one of the greatest live rock bands of the '60s era and beyond! To date, this act has sold no less than 100,000,000 albums worldwide.

The Who's musical instrument contributions, such as the use of the windmill strum, the power chord, and even intentionally using the guitar/amp "noise" called feedback, have been critical in musical development. Away from the music world, the band also inspired others with their pop art-influenced fashion, such as the use of the Union Jack in their appearances. In addition to music and fashion, their guitar-smashing antics in 1964 at the Railway hotel have been listed in *Rolling Stone* mag's "50 Moments That Changed the History of Rock 'n Roll."

Musical Influences

Pink Floyd publicly credited The Who as being their formative influence and even started using the feedback method in their music in 1966.

After visiting the Marshall's music shop in London, even Jimi Hendrix requested an amp setup like Townshend's in 1966. After that, he used the amp in ways that manipulated electronic distortion.

The Beatles, in particular, were close to Keith Moon in the '60s and socialized with him regularly. Sir Paul McCartney thought the band was the most exciting thing since sliced bread. It's said that the song "Helter Skelter" was based on The Who's heavy music style. Finally, even the legendary John Lennon borrowed the guitar style of the single "Pinball Wizard" while strumming the acoustic tune of "Polythene Ham."

Other punk and proto-punk rock bands such as the Clash, the Sex Pistols, and even later, Green Day, have previously cited The Who as a musical influence. This was due to the group's insanely loud-volumed approach during live shows.

Brian May of Queen also said very early on (in The Who's career) that they, in particular, counted them as one of their favorite music groups.

Their Impact

The Who's music has had a significant impact on society. Their songs have tackled important issues and addressed the problems that people face every day. They've provided a voice for the voiceless, and their music has inspired people to stand up for what they believe in.

The Who's music has also helped break down social barriers, and it has brought people together from all walks of life. Thanks to The Who, we've been able to express ourselves freely and share our stories with the world.

Top Quotes from The Who

"Rock music is important to people, because it allows them to escape this crazy world. It allows them not to run away from the problems that are there, but to face up to them, but at the same time sort of DANCE ALL OVER THEM. That's what rock and roll is about." –Pete Townshend

"Keith Moon, God rest his soul, once drove his car through the glass doors of a hotel, driving all the way up to the reception desk, got out and asked for the key to his room." –Pete Townshend

"I have terrible hearing trouble. I have unwittingly helped to invent and refine a type of music that makes its principal proponents deaf." –Pete Townshend ("Top 25 quotes by Pete Townshend," n.d.)

Chapter 9
#2 - The Rolling Stones

The Rolling Stones are truly the greatest rock and roll band in the world and will always be. The last too. Everything that came after them, metal, rap, punk, new wave, pop-rock, you name it...you can trace it all back to the Rolling Stones. They were the first and the last, and no one's ever done it better. –Bob Dylan (from the Traveling Wilburys)

About:

In case you haven't heard, The Rolling Stones are kind of a big deal. They're only the biggest rock band in the world and have been for over 50 years! It's hard to believe that these guys are still going strong, but they show no signs of slowing down anytime soon. So what is it about the Stones that has kept them at the top for so long?

Genre: Folk, rock
Years Active: 1962–present

1960's Discography:

No matter what your age, there's no denying that everyone knows who this band is. They were one of the most influential rock bands established in the '60s and are hot in demand to this very day. Some of their 29 compilation albums, 33 live albums, 30 studio albums, and 121 singles include the following:

Year	Album/Song Name	Chart Position
1965	"I Can't Get No Satisfaction"	UK #1 US #1
1965	*The Rolling Stones, Now!*	US #5
1966	"Paint it Black"	UK #1 US #1
1966	*Big Hits (High Tide and Green Grass)*	UK #3 US #3
1966	*Got Life If You Want It*	US #6
1967	*Their Satanic Majesties Request*	UK #3 US #2

The Band Members of the 1960s. (there were surprisingly more members of The Stones over time than most people realise, and some entries are contentious.)

Member	Position	Years Active	D.O.B	From
Bill Wyman	Backing vocals, bass guitar, lead vocals, keyboards, occasional vocals, and piano	1962 - 1993, 2012	October 24, 1936	Lewisham, London
Brian Jones	Backing vocals, harmonica, keyboards, lead guitar, percussion, rhythm guitar, sitar	1962–1969	February 28, 1942	Cheltenham, London
Caro Little	Drums	1962–1963	December 17, 1938	Shepherd's Bush, London
Charlie Watts	Backing vocals, drums, occasional vocals, percussion	1963–2021	June 2, 1941	London
Colin Golding	Bass guitar	1962–1963	October 24, 1936	Penge, Kent
Dick Taylor	Bass guitar	1962	January 28, 1943	Dartford
Ian Stewart	Organ, percussion, piano	1962–1963 and contract player 1964–1985	July 18, 1938	Pittenweem
Keith Richards	Backing vocals, bass guitar, lead guitar, lead vocals, rhythm guitar	1962–present	December 18, 1943	Dartford

Member	Position	Years Active	D.O.B	From
Mick Jagger	Harmonica, keyboards, lead vocals, backing vocals, rhythm guitar	1962–present	July 26, 1943	Dartford
Mick Taylor	Backing vocals, bass guitar, lead guitar	1969 - 1974, guest 1981, 2012-2014	January 17, 1949	Welwyn Garden City
Ricky Fenson	Bass guitar	1962–1963	May 22, 1945	Chopwell
Tony Chapman	Drums	1962–1963	Unknown	London

Special note: Significant Band Member post 1960s

Ronnie Wood	Rhythm & Lead Guitars	1975 - present	June 1, 1947	Hillington, London

Artistic Facts

- The Stones' logo is inspired by Kali, the Hindu Goddess of Everlasting Energy.
- The cocktail, Tequila Sunrise, was popularized by the band in 1972. This is a result of their cocaine and tequila addictions.
- Mick Jagger is a ballet practitioner.
- The Beatles penned a song for the band.
- On Mick's 75th birthday, he got a big present. Scientists named a group of several stonefly fossils after former and existing Rolling Stones band members. The theme continued when NASA called a rock disturbed by the Mars InSight Lander the "Rolling Stones Rock."

Their Story

The story of Mick Jagger and Keith Richards dates back to 1950 when they were classmates while attending school in Dartford. In 1954, the Jaggers moved five miles away, and Mick established a garage band with his pal, Dick Taylor. The Taylor/Jagger ensemble performed cover songs from bands such as Chuck Berry and Muddy Waters. Richards and Jagger met again in 1961 while both were catching a train. At the encounter, the duo started talking about the Muddy Waters and Chuck Berry albums Jagger was carrying under his arm, and it was not long after that they started jamming together. Richards was a regular in the Jagger household. Later, in 1961, the sessions were moved to Taylor's house, and together with Bob Beckwith and Alan Etherington, they formed a quintet called the Blues Boyz.

In 1962, the quintet read about the Alexis Korner's Blues Incorporated band and decided to send a tape of their best record-ings to Korner. Alexis was suitably impressed and invited the Blues Boyz to visit them at the Ealing Jazz Club, where they were performing. After the encounter, Richards and Jagger started playing with the group for jam sessions.

In May of '62, Brian Jones (then out of band) placed an ad in the Jazz Weekly. Ian Stewart responded first and also secured them a place to practice. Jones and Stewart formed a Chicago Blues band and were joined by Richards, Jagger, and Taylor (after leaving Blues Inc.). Later in the same month, the group was joined by Tony Chapman as drummer, and this completed the band. The story of how the permanent name came about is that Jones was on a phone call to a media outlet, and when asked what the band name was for the article, he quickly said the Rollin' Stones. This was brought on by a Muddy Waters LP lying on the floor, near the phone he was speaking on.

On July 12, 1962, the band officially played their first gig together at the Marquee Club. By then, Taylor had left the band, and in December of the same year, Bill Wyman auditioned and was added as the new bassist. Charlie Watts also joined the Stone's officially on February 2, 1963, after he had been playing with the band at the Ealing Club since January.

The year 1963 was a pretty significant year for the band, as their first UK tour started, which saw an increase in their popularity. Their first manager was Andrew Loog Oldham (ex-Beatles manager). The young lad (only 19 at the time) had to get his mother's consent for contract signing as he could not get an agent's license. As a result, he was signed on by Eric Easton, a booking agent.

At first, Oldham wanted the band to copy the fashion of The Beatles by having them wear suits. Later, he had a change of heart and decided that the Stones should have their own unique style and not copy The Beatles. Later in '63, Stewart parted ways with the group, which was okay in Oldham's eyes as he thought that six band members was too many anyway. Oldham also went on to fudge the genuine ages of the group, so it appeared that they were teenagers (to appeal to the youth). The young manager also later had the Stones pose unsmiling on their first record cover with provocative and raunchy headlines, like "Would you let your daughter marry a Rolling Stone?"

Under Oldham's creative direction, the band's first single to reach the UK Singles Chart (#21) was "Come On." Having a song that charted gave them admission to land a gig at the Outlook Club in July '63, sharing the lineup with the Hollies. The Rolling Stones' first major tour of the United Kingdom also took place later that same year and allowed them to refine their on-stage act. During the tour, Lennon and McCartney sold the rights to their song "I Wanna Be Your Man" to the Stones. It peaked at #12 on the UK Charts.

By 1964, the band had knocked The Beatles off their #1 pedestal in the United Kingdom after two popularity surveys were conducted. Shortly after this, the group's name was officially changed to "The Rolling Stones." An international renaissance followed when Giorgio Gomelsky secured them a permanent band residency at the Crawdaddy Club in London.

The Stones released their second UK-based LP in early '65. It peaked at #1 and #5 in the United States, respectively. During January and February of the same year, the band had played 34 shows for about 100,000 adoring fans in New Zealand and Australia. In May 1965, their first international smash hit "(I Can't Get No) Satisfaction" was recorded and released. On the track, Richards can be heard using his signature guitar riff. This drove the song utilizing a fuzzbox, serving as a scratch track to guide the rest of the band.

The song "Have You Seen Your Mother, Baby, Standing in the Shadow" was released in September 1966. It was the Stone's first official hit to feature a brass section. And to this day, the album's cover remains notable due to the back cover depicting an image of the group dressed in drag.

In early 1967, the Stones released *Between the Buttons*. It managed to secure a #3 spot in the United Kingdom and a #2 rank in the United States. This was also Oldham's final venture with the band as their producer, and he was succeeded by Allen Kline.

In July of '69, Jones mysteriously drowned in the pool at his home in East Sussex, apparently under the heavy influence of booze and drugs – sadly, how very rock and roll. Two days after Jones's passing, the band paid tribute by putting on a free concert in his honor. Jagger read a poem, and thousands of butterflies were released as a tribute. The band went through numerous guitarist auditions and settled on Mick Taylor.

Following contract disputes with Klein, the Stones formed their own record company, called Rolling Stone Records, and released *Sticky Fingers* in March of '71. They jumped on the cultural bandwagon by featuring artwork by Andy Warhol on the cover. *Sticky Fingers* was the first Stones album cover to feature the now-famous Rolling Stone logo; it was a pair of red lips featuring a lapping tongue and was created by John Pasche. Today, it can easily be dubbed the most famous music band logo in history! After the album's release, the Stones went into tax exile and left the United Kingdom for the south of France. It just so happens that despite being assured that they were tax-compliant, they had not paid the UK government for several years and owed them a considerable amount. This saw the band create a financial structure in 1972 to reduce their debt. Sadly, to this day, The Rolling Stones remain in tax exile and can't use the United Kingdom as their primary residence. Funny enough, to date, they've only paid about 1.6% of their 242 million pounds earnings over a 20-year stint ("The Rolling Stones," 2019).

Towards the end of '74, Taylor started feeling restricted in the group. He was the youngest member and was getting irritated with Richards' and Taylor's lack of performance due to drug abuse. After a recording session was already booked in Germany, Taylor decided to leave the band. The band needed a new guitarist, stat. During said recording sessions in Munich, guitarists such as Beck and Gallagher auditioned without even knowing the purpose of the jamming sessions. Sessional artists such as Harvey Mandel and Wayne Perkins also auditioned, but the group wanted the members to all be British. Enter Ronnie Wood; he was everyone's preferred choice. Upon hearing the news, Rod Stewart responded by saying he'd put his head on a block and stated that Wood wouldn't agree to it. As it turned out, Wood officially joined the Stones in 1975 for their tour of the Americas but only became a business partner in early '90.

Throughout the early '70s, the band remained popular with fans, but music critics started losing interest, and the failing record sales were proof thereof. In the mid-'70s, many folks viewed the Stones as has-beens. The odds turned again in their favor in '78 after releasing hits such as "Beast of Burden" and "Miss You." The album *Some Girls*, containing the two songs, reached #2 in the United Kingdom and #1 in the United States. After the success of *Some Girls*, the band released *Emotional Rescue* in the second quarter of 1980. During the album's recording, Richards and Jagger started having fallouts. Richards wanted to tour to promote the album, but Jagger refused. Needless to say, *Emotional Rescue* peaked at #3 in the States. Towards the end of 1982, the band signed a four-album deal with CBS Records, securing them $50,000,000, making it the biggest record deal worldwide.

In 1983, the rift between Jagger and Richards started taking a turn for the worst. Jagger signed a solo contract with CBS and spent the bigger part of 1984 writing for his debut solo record. Jagger also expressed a lack of interest in returning full-time to the Stones. By 1985, Jagger was spending more and more time on solo work. Much of the content on the *Dirty Work* album (released in '86) comprised lyrics penned by Richards. *Dirty Work* was recorded in France, and Jagger was in absentia a lot, driving Richards to keep the sessions going forward sans Jagger.

Jagger's debut solo performance was with David Bowie for "Dancing in the Street." Even though the single reached #7 in the United States and #1 in the United Kingdom, it was earmarked with a tinge of sadness. In December '85, Ian Stewart tragically died of a heart attack in a medical waiting room while seeking assistance for respiratory problems. The band performed a tribute concert in his honor and, a mere 48 hours later, received a Grammy Lifetime Achievement Award.

At the beginning of 1989, the Stones were inducted into the Rock and Roll Hall of fame in the United States, with Stewart receiving a posthumous honor. Richards and Jagger made peace, and the next album, *Steel Wheels*, was released. The album peaked at #3 in the United States and #2 in the United Kingdom. After the success of the Steel Wheels and Urban Jungle tours, the band took a hiatus. Watts released two solo Jazz albums, Wood recorded his fifth solo record, and Wyman released his fourth solo piece. Richards, on the other hand, released a second solo album and toured Argentina and Spain. Jagger also focused on solo work and released his third solo album.

Drug Charges

In January 1967, Jones, Richards, and Jagger came under fire from the authorities for their recreational use of drugs. This saw *News of the World* make a three-part documentary that depicted the alleged tale of LSD parties hosted by The Moody Blues. Apparently, these salacious soirees were attended by music giants such as The Who and even Cream. Two days later, Jagger filed a writ for libel against the publication.

On the 12th of February 1967, the Sussex constabulary raided Richards' home in Redlands. No official arrests were made, but Richards, Fraser and Jagger were charged with drug offenses. Oldham, also in attendance, was afraid of being arrested and fled to the United States. Richards later said that that event became a turning point for the band, where they realized that London was no longer a space where one could be free to explore. It's also rumored that the individual who tipped the police off got the "treatment" and has never walked the same since ...

By May 1967, while Fraser, Jagger, and Richards were arraigned, the police raided Jones' house. He was arrested on the spot and was charged with possession of marijuana. By now, three of the five Rolling Stones faced drug charges. In June, Jagger was sentenced to three months in prison due to possession of amphetamine pills. Richards was sentenced to 365 days in prison for permitting partygoers to use cannabis on his property. One day after Richards and Jagger started serving time, they were released on bail. While the duo awaited their appeal hearings, the Stones recorded "We Love You" as a thank you to their fans! The song's music video starts with the closing of prison doors and allusions to Oscar Wilde's trial. The court decided on the 31st of July that Richards' conviction was to be reduced and overturned, and Jagger's sentence was reduced to a conditional discharge. Jones, on the other hand, had his day in court in November '67, was put on probation for three years, and received a £1,000 fine. Lastly, he was also ordered to seek professional help.

More drug-induced trouble came in '72 during their stint in France. This complicated their plans for their tour of the Pacific the following year. As a result, they were almost banned from playing in Australia and were completely banned in Japan.

The Band Legacy

Since the band got together, they produced many smash hits. It's very easy to see why they are ranked as the #4 best-selling rock band of all time. The group has sold over 240 million records worldwide. They've significantly contributed to the blues "dictionary" with the use of words such as "losing streak" (code word for menstrual period) and have used them extensively in their song library. Mick Jagger will go down in history as the Stone who changed the course of music forever.

In November 1994, the band became the first major group to broadcast over the internet. It would later become the first inclination of what we know as live streaming today, and it opened up the doors of technology to the rest of the world. Throughout the rest of the '90s and early 2000s, the band continued to juggle with solo work, Stones releases, and the intricacies of their personal lives.

In 2012, the band released a book celebrating their 50th anniversary, titled *The Rolling Stones 50*. Their famous logo got a sexy makeover by Shepard Fairey, and Jagger's brother Chris even performed with them. In mid-July 2017, rumors started circulating stating that the band was in the studio recording their first original content in more than a decade. But as of today (2022), it hasn't been released, and the release was delayed due to COVID-19. In August 2021, the world heard that Watts needed surgery and wouldn't participate in the "No Filter" tour. Sadly, Watts passed away on the 24th of August in a London hospital.

Since their inception in the early '60s, The Stones have continued with touring, solo work, and other personal endeavors.

Musical Influences

The Stones and other UK-based bands managed to pique the curiosity and maintain the enthusiasm of US youth in the 60s by exposing them to highly accessible, blues infused music reeking with working-class aches and pains. Indeed, US bluesman Muddy Waters saw his own popularity skyrocket in the States due to him being cited as a major influence on the Stones. This musical exchange between the USA and the UK helped reconnect music lovers in the States with gutsy blues and roots music that originated on their shores, crossed the ditch and made new friends, who then brought it back in a younger, hip form with mop top hair, that the masses lapped up.

Their Impact

The Rolling Stones are widely credited as musical trailblazers in cultural attitudes worldwide. It was during their 1966 North American tour that their concerts, brimming with ecstatic high energy, brought them so much initial attention and, indeed, notoriety. The crowds responded and the boisterous young audiences gave the coppers a hard time with their efforts to maintain control.

Clearly, The Rolling Stones are one of the most popular and important rock bands in history. Their music has had a tremendous impact on society, and their songs continue to be popular more than 50 years later.

Top Quotes from the Stones

"You've got the sun, you've got the moon, and you've got the Rolling Stones." –Keith Richards ("Top 25 quotes by Keith Richards," n.d.)

"Don't take life too seriously, and remember; it's just a passing fad." –Mick Jagger ("Quotes about Mick Jagger," n.d.)

Chapter 10
#1 - The Beatles

The reason I'm a musician is because of the Beatles. They
conquered the world with their songs, and therefore gave
permission, a decade younger, to try the same thing...
We owe a lot to the Beatles, they really were an amazing influence
on all of our lives. –Sting (from the Police)

About:

It's hard to believe that there was a time before The Beatles. John, Paul, George, and Ringo completely changed the music scene, and their songs are still popular today. But who were these enigmatic musicians? How did they come together? What was their creative process? The Beatles are a big deal: this brief story hopes to shed at least some light on the most important of your Beatles-related questions!

Genre: Pop, psychedelic rock, blues
Years Active: 1960–1970

Discography:

No surprises, unchallenged at the Top-of-the-Pops – with their cheeky grins, uber catchy tunes and sporting their parent-displeasing, mop-top hairstyles – sits the "the Fab Four,". Many young girls had dreams of becoming a Mrs. Beatle, but at least all of them got to enjoy great music. While there is conjecture, most pop aficionados agree the lads released 54 compilation albums, six live albums, 21 studio albums, 22 video albums, and 63 singles. I'll cover most of what is considered the canon of their album work below and toss in some of the singles – and even stretch the 60s focus of this book to include their 1970s finalé album. Here's just a sample of the most recognizable of their fine works and their stellar chat positions in the US & UK:

The British Invasion (the Bands) - The Best 60's Pop & Rock Music

Year	Album/Song Name	Chart Position
1962	"Love Me Do"	UK #4 US #1
1963	*Please Please Me*	UK #1
1963	*With The Beatles*	UK #1
1963	"She Loves You"	UK #1 US #1
1964	*Introducing The Beatles*	US #2
1964	*A Hard Day's Night*	UK #1
1964	*The Beatles' Second Album*	US #1
1964	"Eight Days a Week"	US #1
1964	*Something New*	US #2
1964	*Beatles For Sale*	UK #1
1965	*Help!*	UK #1 US #1
1965	*Beatles '65*	US #1
1965	*Beatles VI*	US #1
1965	Rubber Soul	UK #1 US #1
1966	"Paperback Writer"	UK #1 US #1
1966	*Yesterday And Today*	US #1
1966	*Revolver*	UK #1 US #1
1967	"Penny Lane"	UK #2 US #1
1967	*Sgt. Petter's Lonely Hearts Club Band*	UK #1 US #1
1968	*The Beatles (The White Album)*	UK #1 US #1

Year	Album/Song Name	Chart Position
1968	"Hey Jude"	UK #1 US #1
1968	Magical Mystery Tour	UK #31 US #1
1969	*Abbey Road*	UK #1 US #1
1969	*Yellow Submarine*	UK #3 US #2
1970	*Let It Be*	UK #1 US #1

The Band Members

We only have space to take a close look at The Beatles classic line up; George, John, Ringo and Paul. We'll mention the other fine lads too, but the focus will be on the Fab 4. The disbandment of the group was a complex story, which we'll touch on below. There were many rumours and whispers as to why The Beatles broke up; some say it was fallout due to their manager's death (1967), some say it was the Lennon-Ono effect (1969), or was it perhaps the fact that McCartney said it was Lennon and Lennon said it was McCartney? There were a couple of notable changes in the early line-up, until they settled on the classic band members the world fell in love with - here goes:

The British Invasion (the Bands) - The Best 60's Pop & Rock Music

Member	Position	Years Active	D.O.B	From
John Lennon	Bass guitar, harmonica, keyboards, vocals	1960–1969	October 9, 1940	Liverpool
George Harrison	Bass, guitars, keyboards, sitar, vocals	1960–1969	February 25, 1943	Liverpool
Paul McCartney	Vocals, bass guitar, drums, keyboards	1960–1969	June 18, 1942	Walton, Liverpool
Ringo Starr	Drums, percussion, vocals	1962–1970	July 7, 1940	Dingle, Liverpool
Stuart Sutcliffe	Bass, Vocals	1960-	June 23, 1940	Edinburgh, Scotland
Pete Best	Drums, Vocals	1960-1962	November 24, 1941	Madras, (British) India
Chas Newby	Bass	1960	June 18, 1941	Liverpool, England
Tommy Moore	Drums	1960	September 12, 1931	Liverpool, England
Jimmie Nicol	Drums (touring)	1964	August 3, 1939	London, England
Norman Chapman	Drums	1960	August 5, 1937	England

Artistic Facts

- Lennon's second wife and McCartney's first went to school together at Sarah Lawrence College.
- When talking about The Beatles, the media of the day frequently mentioned them in order of joining the band, which is: John, Paul, George, and Ringo.
- Before the band was signed by Capitol Records (US), they were rejected by five other record labels.
- Towards the end of 1970, the group had sold 500,million albums.

- The Guinness Book of World Records estimates that the band's sales totaled $545,000,000, between '63 to '74.

Their Story

The Fab 4 had humble beginnings like most bands, but their musical and social influence grew rapidly and wildly until they also became known as "Liverpool's Favourite Sons" and even "The World's Greatest Band." An irreversible turning point in their juggernaut career occurred on April 4, 1964 when The Beatles created modern history by being the first band to hold all the top 5 positions on the USA Billboard Hot 100 singles charts at the same time with "Please Please Me", "I Want to Hold Your Hand", "She Loves You", "Twist and Shout" and "Can't Buy Me Love". Quite an amazing feat.

But it all began when, at the age of 16, Lennon formed a skiffle group with a few of his friends while attending Quarry Bank High School in Liverpool. Skiffle is a type of folk music blending blues, American folk and jazz commonly performed with a mix of some-what improvised instruments as well as traditional manufactured instruments. Before any public performances they were briefly called the Blackjacks but the name was changed to the Quar-rymen for their first gigs. McCartney met Lennon in July '57 and shortly after joined the band in the capacity of rhythm guitarist. In early 1958, McCartney invited George Harrison (15 at the time) to come and watch the band play. Harrison auditioned for John, who was suitably impressed, but Lennon thought that he was too young at the time. A month later, after persistence from McCart-ney, Harrison performed with the band, and this saw him being offered a permanent spot as lead guitarist.

By early 1959, the rest of Lennon's friends from school had

left the group. The three guitarists changed their name to Johnny and the Moondogs and performed as often as they could secure a session drummer. At the time fellow art student Stuart Sutcliffe sold one of his own paintings and bought a bass guitar. He joined the ensemble in 1960. Sutcliffe suggested that they change their name to "Beatals" as a tribute to the Crickets and Buddy Holly. The name was used until May and was changed to the "Silver Beetles." In July, the name was once again reshaped to that of "Silver Beatles," and by July, the name was dropped to "The Beatles."

In the mid-'60s, the band hired Pete Best as a drummer. Only four days later, the now five-piece ensemble departed for Hamburg under contract from Bruno Koschmider for three and a half months. Their first residency was at Koschmider's Indra Club. After the club had to be closed down due to noise complaints, Koschmider moved them to Kaiserkeller Club. The first hint of trouble came when Koschmider learned that the group had secretly performed at rival venue Top Ten Club. They were in breach of their contract, and Koschmider served them with one month's termination notice and reported to the authorities that Harrison was still underage. Harrison was later deported, while McCartney and Best were incarcerated on arson charges. Why? It just so happens that the pair lit a condom on fire in a concrete hallway. Later, Lennon returned home, and Sutcliffe remained behind with his German fiancé, who also took the first semi-professional photos of the band.

The next two years were hectic for The Beatles with band members coming and going between Germany and the UK, fighting illnesses, some run ins with the law in Germany and indeed German immigration. You see, they had an on-off residency in Hamburg and started using the stimulant Preludin to keep their energy levels up. It was in 1961 that Sutcliffe was the first person to get the existential "exi" haircut that was later adopted by his fellow bandmates. Shortly after, Sutcliffe quit the band to resume his art studies in Germany, and McCartney took up the bass position. The now four-person group was contracted by Bert Kaempfert until mid-1962 and was used as Tony Sheridan's backup band for a range of recordings under the Polydor record label. They recorded the single "My Bonnie" in June, and it was released a few months later. It managed to peak at #32 in Germany.

Back home, the Merseybeat movement was started, and the band's popularity increased. But, with this, the band became bored of appearing at the same club every night in Hamburg during their second residency. During one of their performances at The Cavern Club, they made the acquaintance of Brian Epstein, a music columnist and record-store owner. During the next few months, he was appointed as their manager. Epstein made it his mission to release the band early from their contact with Kaempfert. Later, he negotiated a release one month early from the expiry date, with the condition that they attend one last recording session in Hamburg. The band returned in April and were met at the airport. It turns out that Sutcliffe had died a day earlier in Hamburg at the age of 21 from a brain hemorrhage. The band was rejected by Decca Records and three months later signed by George Martin to EMI.

The group's first recording session took place on June 6, 1962 at EMI's studios. Martin immediately voiced his dissatisfaction with Best's drumming and wanted to use a session drummer instead. Interestingly enough, The Beatles were already thinking about dismissing Best, and he was replaced by Ringo Starr. By December 1962, the band finished their last residency in Hamburg.

In 1963, the four-piece band agreed that going forward,

everyone would contribute to vocals on records. McCartney and Lennon had formed a strong songwriting team, and as The Beatles' success grew, their partnership grew stronger. By then, Epstein had advised the band that if they wanted to be taken seriously, they needed to stop eating, smoking, and swearing on stage.

In February '63, the band recorded 10 songs in one session for their debut album *Please Please Me*. In March of the same year, the album was released, and it became one of 11 consecutive records released in the United Kingdom to reach #1. The Beatles' third single, "From Me to You," was released in April, and their fourth, titled "She Loves You," came out in August. The latter was on the album that would later become the fastest-selling album in the United Kingdom at the time. It managed to sell 750,000 copies in less than a month. It was also their first hit to sell 1 million copies and retained the #1 best-selling spot for record sales in the United Kingdom until 1978.

The term "Beatlemania" was first coined when the group responded with grace to their rising popularity, making them more appealing to their adoring fans. The band toured their home country three times in '63 and were met by screaming (and crying) female fans. During these tours, they were not seen by music execs as a top billing band, but by audience demand, they managed to unseat artists such as Roy Orbinson, Chris Montez, and Tommy Roe. At the time, no other UK act had accomplished the same while on tour with US-based bands.

In October, they embarked on a tour of Sweden, and when they returned home, hundreds of fans waited for them at Heathrow Airport. A day after arriving home, they began their fourth tour in nine months in the United Kingdom, and by mid-November, the police had to control the screaming crowds with water hoses before a concert in Plymouth.

Epstein took a demo tape of "I Want to Hold Your Hand" to

Capitol Records in the United States. As it turns out, this was the start of big things. The song started garnering air-time in mid-December '63. Other taped versions were shared between various US radio stations that dramatically increased demand, so much so that the single's release was brought forward by three weeks. It sold 1 million copies and became a #1 hit in the States by mid-January 1964. The band departed for a tour of the United States on February 7. The tour happened a few months after JFK's assassination the previous November. It is said that with the arrival of The Beatles in the United States came some happiness and excitement after the sadness of losing their then-President. Even though the band was ridiculed by some for their hairstyles, it started a youth revolution. In addition to this, the band's touring of the United States paved the way for other UK artists to join the movement in what is known as the British Invasion. The Beatles had successfully paved the way for bands such as The Animals, The Kinks, and the Stones to achieve success in the United States.

Controversy came in 1966 when US religious groups and even the Ku Klux Klan were up in arms about Lennon's comments against Christianity. His comments weren't pertinently noticed in the United Kingdom, but after a US teenage magazine posted his comments, the Vatican issued a protest. Countries such as Spain, Holland, and even South Africa imposed bans on their record sales. In response, Epstein said that Lennon's words were taken out of context, and Lennon's comments reflected how their fans viewed them. Lennon himself tried to walk them back and soften the blow of his invective with something of a public apology. However, what Lennon is actually quoted to have said originally is rather unambiguous –

"Christianity will go. It will vanish and shrink. I needn't argue about that; I'm right and I'll be proved right. We're more popular than Jesus now; I don't know which will go first – rock 'n' roll or

Christianity. Jesus was all right but his disciples were thick and ordinary. It's them twisting it that ruins it for me."

The result? Records were burned, tour bans were instituted, The Pope protested, and passionate public demonstrations ensued. The Beatles went from strength to strength and Christianity didn't fade away - it is still widely adhered to and growing around the globe. I guess we must admit, love him though many of us do, that John was wrong on at least that one point.

In December of '67, the EP for the *Magical Mystery Tour* soundtrack was released. It was the first inclination of a double EP released in the United Kingdom. In the first three weeks of release, the album had set an unprecedented record for the highest-grossing initial sales of any Capitol Record EP. To date, it's also the only Capitol compilation to be adopted in their official canon of studio records.

After the release of many singles between '68–'70, McCartney filed suit for the disbandment of the group's contractual partnership in December of 1970. During this time, each band member continued working on their solo careers. Many legal disputes have occurred since, with the dissolution being only formalized in December 1974. This came after Lennon signed the paperwork while on vacation in Florida.

The world was shocked, when in December 1980, Lennon was assassinated outside of his apartment in New York leaving a huge musical legacy and distraught and grieving fans. The Beatles were inducted into the Rock and Roll Hall of Fame in 1988 with Starr and Harrison in attendance, supporting Yoko Ono (Lennon's widow) and their two sons. McCartney declined the invitation to attend, stating irreconcilable business differences and not wanting to feel fake. In 1981, Capitol/EMI settled the decade-long lawsuit filed by The Beatles over royalties. This meant that previously unreleased material would now see the light of day.

The Band Legacy

The Beatles have been credited as the music group that broke free from creative constraints and emerged with something original and unique. No other band has been more creative, distinctive, or revolutionary in that regard.

With the band's arrival in '64 in the States, they initiated what is now known as the "era of albums", Beatlemania and with it the British Invasion in the United States was begun.

The group will forever go down in music history as true cultural icons from the United Kingdom.

Musical Influences

The Beatles' commercial success and musical innovations have ignited creativity in other musicians the world over. They had such a big impact that the WABC radio program director forbade his radio presenters to play anything pre-Beatle era in 1968.

With their August 1965 concert at The Shea Stadium in Queens, NY, they attracted the largest audience ever for its time. It's estimated that no less than 55,600 people were in attendance that day. A 50 minute documentary film was made about that concert

Their fashion sense and haircuts became an insignia of youth rebellion and had a major impact on clothing and hairstyles globally.

With Beatlemania, the group has forever changed how we listen to music and how it formed our lives. The band's popularity had grown into what was seen as the epitome of sociocultural movement in the '60s and '70s. Not only had they raised awareness in political and social areas, but they fueled the interest in bohemianism.

After Lennon's controversial interview in 1966, where he said that The Beatles were more popular than Jesus, the band had felt the burning need from society to walk the narrow path. Thus, they evolved their image to spread what they felt were more universal messages of hope, higher consciousness, and wisdom.

Their Impact

When The Beatles first arrived on the scene in the early 1960s, they were greeted with mixed reactions. Some people loved their music and unique style, while others found them too loud and disruptive. Over time, however, The Beatles became arguably the most influential and popular band in modern music history.

Their music changed the way people thought about music and inspired others to create their own unique sounds. The Beatles also had a profound impact on social customs and norms. Their songs spoke to a generation of young people searching for meaning and purpose in their lives.

The Beatles helped define a new era in which youth culture played a central role. They showed that it was possible to set your own course amidst waves of opposition: to be super creative and expressive while still maintaining professionalism and developing a keen music business acumen.

Top Quotes from The Beatles

"Everything will be okay in the end. If it's not okay, it's not the end." –John Lennon (Adams, n.d.)

"Music is like a psychiatrist. You can tell your guitar things that you can't tell people. And it will answer you with things people can't tell you." -Paul McCartney (RollingStone, *"Paul McCartney Looks Back: The Rolling Stone Interview"* 2016)

"If you don't know where you're going, any road'll take you there"

— *George Harrison ("George Harrison> Quotes," n.d.)*

"Everything the government touches turns to crap" –Ringo Starr ("Ringo Starr Quotes," n.d.)

"Life is what happens when you are busy making other plans" – John Lennon *("Top 25 quotes by John Lennon," n.d.)*

"My grandkids always beat me at (the game) Rock Band. And I say 'You may beat me at rock band, but I made the original records. So shut up.'" –Paul McCartney (cat1052271, n.d.)

"The Beatles saved the world from boredom." —*George Harrison ("George Harrison> Quotes," n.d.)*

"I'd like to end up sort of unforgettable." " –Ringo Starr *("Ringo Starr Quotes," n.d.)*

Conclusion: The Beat Goes On!

The British Invasion was the most important event of my life. I was in New Jersey, and the night I saw the Beatles changed everything. I had seen Elvis before, and he had done nothing for me, but these guys were in a band. –Stevie van Zandt (from Bruce Springsteen's E Street Band)

The British Invasion music of the 1960s had a significant impact on American popular culture and, by extension, the world! The British bands that toured America and released records in the early 1960s helped introduce a new sound and style to American audiences. This new music was heavily influenced by the blues, rock and roll, and R&B music originally imported to the UK from the USA but infused with an across-the-pond flavour that made it so popular in the UK and lapped up by kids in America as something new and fresh and totally hip. Some of the most influential British Invasion bands of the 60s include The Beatles, The Rolling Stones, The Kinks, and The Who.

The British Invasion was a musical movement in the early

1960s when a wave of British rock and roll artists came to the United States and achieved immense popularity. The invasion is said to have begun on January 18, 1964, when The Beatles debuted on *The Ed Sullivan Show*. The crowd was pent up with expectancy - and they just went wild for the Fab 4! The Invasion, by all intents and purposes, was going to be a huge success. And other so-called beat-bands followed in their wake until 1966-67. But in this book we've charted together the Invasion of the best British bands of the whole decade! What a tour de-force!

The arrival of these bands in America helped to usher in a new era of rock and roll. Their music was louder, more energetic, and more rebellious and aggressive than the pop music popular in the 1950s. They also introduced new fashion styles and hairstyles that quickly became popular among American youth. The British Invasion music helped create a new sense of identity and culture among American teenagers, and it continues to be popular among music fans today. Thanks in part to the British Invasion, rock and roll became the dominant form of popular music in America for the next several decades.

The impact of the British Invasion was far-reaching. It not only transformed American pop music but also helped break down cultural barriers between the United States and Britain. In addition, it led to the development of more creative and experimental forms of rock music. As a result, the British Invasion is often seen as a watershed moment in rock and roll history.

The '60s were a time of upheaval and change across society.

Artists like Jimi Hendrix and Aretha Franklin helped to show that black artists could be just as successful as white artists. They showed that the color of your skin didn't matter. In turn, Janis Joplin and Tina Turner showed that women could be powerful, successful, and do anything they wanted to.

The music of the '60s also helped change the way people

thought about politics and social issues. Bob Dylan and Joan Baez are famous for writing songs about important political issues. They helped raise awareness about things like the Vietnam War and the Civil Rights Movement.

The music of the British Invasion lives on in the hearts of the fans of classic pop and rock! Innumerable contemporary artists in almost every language on the face of the globe continue to cover and popularize these amazing songs from these extraordinary musical pioneers, ensuring that the legacy will thrive for many years to come.

Thanks, 60s music! You rock! :-)

Bonus Section

THANK YOU!

...so much for getting your copy of **The British Invasion (The Bands) The Best 60s Pop & Rock Music.** If you enjoyed the book, *I'd love for you to leave a rating and review.*

It really helps!

Get your FREE BONUS Chapter

Be sure to download your **FREE BONUS chapter - the next 10 bands in the Top 20**. Go to the BOOKS page on https://www.pjchambers.org/.

The Next Book In the Invasion Series

Also, if you liked this, keep your eyes peeled for the next book in the series: **The British Invasion (The Soloists) The**

Best 60s Pop & Rock Music. If you love songs from singers like Dusty Springfield, Petula Clark, Tom Jones, Marianne Faithful and others, **you'll love** the next installment of The Invasion Series.

Help Me Out! Join The Cool Kids

If you have ideas and suggestions for updating content, corrections, oversights, or additional books you'd like to read - please just jump on my website and send me a message. I'd love to hear from you.

https://www.pjchambers.org/

Peace out!
PJ Chambers

References

Adams, K. (n.d.). *30 John Lennon quotes ideas*. Pinterest. https://za.pinterest.com/cooch51/john-lennon-quotes/

The Animals. (n.d.). Discogs. https://www.discogs.com/artist/269090-The-Animals

The Animals - Famous quotes and quotations. (n.d.). Music With Ease. https://www.musicwithease.com/the-animals-quotes.html

The Animals | Rock & Roll Hall of Fame. (n.d.). Rock & Roll Hall of Fame. https://www.rockhall.com/inductees/animals

The Animals artistfacts. (n.d.). Songfacts. https://www.songfacts.com/facts/the-animals

Band Cream quotes. (n.d.). Picture Quotes. http://www.picturequotes.com/band-cream-quotes

References

The Beatles. (2019, January 13). Wikipedia. https://en.wikipedia.org/wiki/The_Beatles

The Beatles artistfacts. (2018). Songfacts. https://www.songfacts.com/facts/the-beatles

The Beatles discography. (2019, December 1). Wikipedia. https://en.wikipedia.org/wiki/The_Beatles_discography

Blues quotes. (n.d.). Picture Quotes. http://www.picturequotes.com/blues-quotes/4

Bob Dylan quote. (n.d.). AZ Quotes. https://www.azquotes.com/quote/1087065

cat1052271. (n.d.). *Famous quotes - Paul McCartney.* Wattpad. https://www.wattpad.com/483750263-famous-quotes-paul-mccartney

Clash, J. (2019, July 15). A no-holds-barred interview with the Animals' Eric Burdon, still as feisty as ever. *Forbes.* https://www.forbes.com/sites/jimclash/2019/07/15/a-no-holds-barred-interview-with-the-animals-eric-burdon-still-as-feisty-as-ever/?sh=4fdfb6cd325e

Cream (band). (2020, November 8). Wikipedia. https://en.wikipedia.org/wiki/Cream_(band)

Cream discography. (2021, December 8). Wikipedia. https://en.wikipedia.org/wiki/Cream_discography

References

Cream Song Facts. (n.d.). Songfacts. https://www.songfacts.com/facts/cream

Dale, R. (2018, January 18). Small Faces launch legal action against a West End musical based on them. *The Sun*. https://www.thesun.co.uk/tvandshowbiz/5367514/small-faces-launch-musical-legal-action/

Dave Davies quotes. (n.d.). BrainyQuote. https://www.brainyquote.com/quotes/dave_davies_671821?src=t_question_mark

Domino, M. (2013, May 9). Small wonders. *The Paris Review*. https://www.theparisreview.org/blog/2013/05/09/small-wonders/

Eddie Van Halen quotes. (n.d.). PICTUREQUOTES. http://www.picturequotes.com/eddie-van-halen-quotes

Eric Burdon. (n.d.). PBS. https://www.pbs.org/opb/thesixties/topics/culture/reflections_1.html

Eric Burdon biography, songs, & albums. (n.d.). All Music. https://www.allmusic.com/artist/eric-burdon-mn0000154548/biography

Eric Clapton quote. (n.d.). AZ Quotes. https://www.azquotes.com/quote/1462020

Fricke, D. (2016, August 10). Paul McCartney Looks Back. *Rolling Stone*. https://www.rollingstone.com/music/music-features/paul-mccartney-looks-back-the-rolling-stone-interview-102797/

References

George Harrison Quotes. (n.d.) Goodreads.com. *https://www. goodreads.com/author/quotes/20108.George_Harrison*

Ginger Baker. (2019, August 29). Wikipedia. https://en.wikipedia. org/wiki/Ginger_Baker

Ginger Baker quotes. (n.d.). Contactmusic.com. https://www. contactmusic.com/ginger-baker/quotes

Gordon Edwards discography - RYM/Sonemic. (n.d.). Rate Your Music. https://rateyourmusic.com/artist/gordon-edwards

Graeme Edge quotations. (n.d.). QuoteTab. https://www.quotetab. com/quotes/by-graeme-edge

Hewitt, P. (1995). *Small Faces: The young mods' forgotten story.* Acid Jazz Books.

History of the Animals. (n.d.). Animals III. https://animals3.com/ history-of-the-band.php

Ian McLagan quotes. (n.d.). BrainyQuote. https://www. brainyquote.com/quotes/ian_mclagan_685143

Jimmy Page quotes. (n.d.). Quotefancy. https://quotefancy.com/ jimmy-page-quotes

Joe Walsh quotes. (n.d.). BrainyQuote. https://www.brainyquote. com/authors/joe-walsh-quotes

Justin Hayward quotes. (n.d.). BrainyQuote. https://www. brainyquote.com/authors/justin-hayward-quotes

References

Kiger, P. (2013, February 5). *Reg Presley: 10 facts about the rocker who gave us "Wild Thing."* AARP. https://blog.aarp.org/legacy/reg-presley-10-facts-about-the-rocker-who-gave-us-wild-thing

The Kinks. (2021, May 26). Wikipedia. https://en.wikipedia.org/wiki/The_Kinks

The Kinks artistfacts. (n.d.). Songfacts. https://www.songfacts.com/facts/the-kinks

The Kinks discography. (2022, February 12). Wikipedia. https://en.wikipedia.org/wiki/The_Kinks_discography

Laing, R. (2021, November 22). *Sting on the Beatles: "They conquered the world with their own songs, and therefore gave permission to a younger generation to try the same thing."* Musicradar. https://www.musicradar.com/news/sting-beatles-paul-mccartney

List of the Kinks band members. (2022, January 10). Wikipedia. https://en.wikipedia.org/wiki/List_of_the_Kinks_band_members

List of the Yardbirds members. (2021, October 16). Wikipedia. https://en.wikipedia.org/wiki/List_of_the_Yardbirds_members

London, A. (2021, April 9). *The Yardbirds.* Song Meanings + Facts. https://www.songmeaningsandfacts.com/the-yardbirds/

The Moody Blues. (n.d.). Songfacts. https://www.songfacts.com/facts/the-moody-blues

Puterbaugh, P. (1988, July 15). The British Invasion: From the

References

Beatles to the Stones, the sixties belonged to Britain. *Rolling Stone*. https://www.rollingstone.com/feature/the-british-invasion-from-the-beatles-to-the-stones-the-sixties-belonged-to-britain-244870/

Quotes about British Invasion: Top 18 British invasion quotes from famous authors. (n.d.). More Famous Quotes. https://www.morefamousquotes.com/topics/quotes-about-british-invasion/

Quotes about Eric Clapton (55 quotes). (2019). Quote Master. https://www.quotemaster.org/Eric+Clapton

Quotes about Mick Jagger (82 quotes). (n.d.). Quote Master. https://www.quotemaster.org/Mick+Jagger

Quote by Ozzy Osbourne. (n.d.). Goodreads. https://www.goodreads.com/quotes/506538-as-far-as-we-were-concerned-we-were-just-a

The Rolling Stones discography. (2019). Wikipedia. https://en.wikipedia.org/wiki/The_Rolling_Stones_discography

Ringo Starr Quotes. (n.d.) BrainyQuote. https://www.brainyquote.com/authors/ringo-starr-quotes

Rolling Stone. Exclusive: The complete text of Bruce Springsteen's SXSW keynote address. (2012, March 28). *Rolling Stone*. https://www.rollingstone.com/music/music-news/exclusive-the-complete-text-of-bruce-springsteens-sxsw-keynote-address-86379

Ronnie Montrose quote. (n.d.). AZ Quotes. https://www.azquotes.com/quote/910245

References

Shapiro, M. (2010, September 15). *The story behind the song: Wild Thing by The Troggs.* LOUDER Sound. https://www.louder sound.com/features/the-story-behind-the-song-wild-thing-by-the-troggs

Slash quotes. (n.d.). BrainyQuote. https://www.brainyquote.com/authors/slash-quotes

Small Faces artistfacts. (n.d.). Songfacts. https://www.songfacts.com/facts/small-faces

Small Faces fun facts, quotes and tweets. (n.d.). Contactmusic.com. https://www.contactmusic.com/small-faces/quotes

Snow, M. (2013, February 5). Reg Presley: "I must learn to swear more often" – a classic feature from the vaults. *The Guardian.* https://www.theguardian.com/music/2013/feb/05/from-rocks-backpages-troggs-reg-presley

Something Else! *"There was a connection": Eric Burdon on how the Animals' "House of the Rising Sun" transformed Bob Dylan.* (2013, February 9). https://somethingelsereviews.com/2013/02/09/there-was-a-connection-eric-burdon-says-the-animals-house-of-the-rising-sun-transformed-bob-dylan/

Steffen, L. (2021, September 14). The best 60s slang to get your groove on. *Babbel Magazine.* https://www.babbel.com/en/maga zine/best-1960s-slang

Streit, K. (2018, December 19). *30 cool and crazy facts you may not know about The Rolling Stones.* Simplemost. https://www.simplemost.com/rolling-stones-facts/

References

Top 25 quotes by Bob Dylan (of 872). (n.d.). AZ Quotes. https://www.azquotes.com/author/4273-Bob_Dylan

Top 25 quotes by John Lennon (of 624). (n.d.). AZ Quotes. https://www.azquotes.com/author/8717-John_Lennon

Top 25 quotes by Keith Richards (of 164). (n.d.). AZ Quotes. https://www.azquotes.com/author/12308-Keith_Richards

Top 25 quotes by Pete Townshend (of 122). (n.d.). AZ Quotes. https://www.azquotes.com/author/14747-Pete_Townshend

Top 26 quotes about the British Invasion: Famous quotes & sayings about the British Invasion. (n.d.). Quotes Stats. https://quotestats.com/topic/quotes-about-the-british-invasion/

Top 68 Van Zandt quotes: Famous quotes & sayings about Van Zandt. (n.d.). Quotes Stats. https://quotestats.com/topic/van-zandt-quotes/

Top 100 quotes about Oasis: Famous quotes & sayings about Oasis. (n.d.). Quotes Stats. https://quotestats.com/topic/quotes-about-oasis/

Top Pete Townshend quotes & sayings. (n.d.). The Famous People. https://quotes.thefamouspeople.com/pete-townshend-2551.php

The Beatles vs. The Ku Klux Klan: How it change the band forever more. (2021, October 2). *https://faroutmagazine.co.uk/the-beatles-vs-the-ku-klux-klan/*

References

The Troggs. (2022, January 24). Wikipedia. https://en.wikipedia.org/wiki/The_Troggs

The Troggs history. (n.d.). The Troggs. https://www.thetroggs.co.uk/bio

The Who. (2019, April 1). Wikipedia. https://en.wikipedia.org/wiki/The_Who

Who are the next Rock & Roll Hall of Famers? (n.d.). Future Rock Legends. https://futurerocklegends.com/Artist/The_Small_Faces-The_Faces/

The Who artistfacts. (n.d.). Songfacts. https://www.songfacts.com/facts/the-who

The Who discography. (2019, October 12). Wikipedia. https://en.wikipedia.org/wiki/The_Who_discography

Williams, R. (n.d.). *The Animals | Members, songs, & facts.* Encyclopedia Britannica. https://www.britannica.com/topic/The-Animals

World's best The Kinks quotes images to share and download. (n.d.). QuotesLyfe. https://www.quoteslyfe.com/author/The-Kinks-quotes

About the Author

PJ Chambers is a music nutter, writer, actor, cartoonist, encourager, and all-round normal guy. On his musical side, he has been a session "muso" in the studio and with professional bands, and has written and published many songs. Apparently, he remembers (and loves) the 60s(!) where his musical passion was formed. To PJ, music is one of those essential elements that makes life worth ... living. As he has gone on many musical mystery tours himself, he hopes that you, who was born to be wild, will choose to come with him on a magic carpet ride. So please join him on the last freedom-bound moped out of oblivion through the pages of the inside stories of rock n roll, love, peace, joy and happiness that only the greatest music by the best musicians can provide. "If music be the food of love, play on; Give me excess of it" (Shakespeare)

Printed in Great Britain
by Amazon

13991089R00093